ASTROLOGY
D I C T I O N A R Y

EVERYTHING YOU NEED TO
KNOW ABOUT THE WESTERN
AND EASTERN ZODIACS

COMPREHENSIVE EXPLANATIONS
OF HOROSCOPES, PERSONAL
CHARACTER, AND RELATIONSHIPS

Antonia Beattie

THUNDER BAY
P · R · E · S · S
SAN DIEGO, CALIFORNIA

Ye stars,
that are the poetry
of heaven!

—LORD BYRON

CONTENTS

INTRODUCTION

Astrology Around the World

All astrology systems grew out of the need to fix a calendar for agriculture; the agricultural "year" itself then became punctuated by religious festivals. These festivals mark turning points of the year—the right time to start planting, or to move animals to higher or lower pastures, for instance. Europe, the Middle East, and the Indian subcontinent all developed systems that originated in what is now Iraq.

Western astrology moved from Iraq into Egypt, then to the Greek and Roman empires. Chinese astrology started in the areas around the Yellow River. Central American astrology originated with the Maya and Toltec people and was developed further by the Aztecs; some of this permeated Native American astrology, although local myths and local observation of the sky also played a part in the Native American tradition. African astrology uses Egyptian and North African studies of animal marks on sandy or soft soils, as well as observations of the heavens. Norse and Celtic astrology are an amalgam of pagan myths and measurements of the sun's movement.

Ancient people believed that planetary movements signaled events such as floods, good and bad harvests, or wars with neighboring tribes, so the predictive aspects of astrology soon followed. Early astrologers believed that the position of the planets rising over the horizon or at the top of the sky at a person's birth foretold the potential character and destiny of that person. This kind of thinking was never applied to "common" people—it was only used for royal babies and the sons of military, religious, or court leaders.

The popularization of astrology in our own age came about through just this kind of royal horoscope. In 1930, a British astrologer outlined and interpreted a chart for the infant Princess Margaret for an article in a national newspaper. This article was so popular that the editor asked the astrologer if he could do something for the general public. He did—and newspaper astrology took off. The original article also sparked interest in more detailed forms of astrology.

This dictionary gives an overview of many different astrology traditions so that you can look up your astrological sign in Western, Chinese, and Native American astrology and perhaps gain additional insight into your own personal character profile. Also, if you want to know what your month of birth means, not only in Western astrology but also in Chinese, Vedic, Native American, Celtic tree, or Norse runic astrology, here is your opportunity to find out.

The first part of the book tells you about a host of ancient and modern types of astrology. To find the signs that apply to you, select the month in which you were born in the A–Z section. Look at the first day of the month. This shows which signs were in operation in all the systems on the first day of each month, so if you happen to have been born on the first of the month, all these will be yours.

If you were born on any other day, you will have to track through the calendar to see which apply to you. You might like to have a pen and paper handy for this. For example, if you were born on January 25, this would be your picture:

Western astrology:	Aquarius
Chinese astrology:	Receptive earth, Ox
Vedic astrology:	Makara, like Capricorn
Mansion 25:	Purva Bhadra
Native American astrology:	Otter, Butterfly clan
West African astrology:	The Baobab Tree
Celtic tree astrology:	Cypress
Norse runic astrology:	Pertho

The information in *Astrology Dictionary* will help you gain a deeper understanding of who you are and how you relate to the world. You will acquire a richer appreciation of your own and others' uniqueness, and how the differences between people can complement and support each other.

Western Astrology

If you can put yourself into the minds of those who lived before the solar system was discovered, it is easy to see why they believed that the Sun traveled around the Earth—we now know that it is, in fact, the other way around.

This apparent pathway of the Sun around the Earth is called the ecliptic. The constellations of stars that lie along the ecliptic are the signs of the zodiac we are familiar with—from Aries to Pisces. The signs run in this order because the tropical zodiac starts at the spring equinox in the Northern Hemisphere—March 21. This becomes the start of the sign of Aries; the rest of the signs follow, from Taurus through to Pisces.

The Moon and the planets also travel close to this path, although they cross up and down over it from time to time. For the sake of simplicity, astrologers call everything a planet, including the Sun and the Moon. Planets are at various angles to one another, depending upon where they are along this line—astrologers call these angles aspects. If, for instance, Venus was on one side of the Earth while Saturn was around the other side, this would be described as an opposition between Venus and Saturn.

Astrologers work from charts that show the position of the planets, the aspects, and many other important features. A natal—or birth—chart is set for a specific date, time, and place of a person's birth; it is a stylized illustration of the sky at the moment of a person's birth. Such a chart can also apply to the birth of a country, a city, a business, a marriage, or any other kind of enterprise. By plotting the movement of the planets against the natal chart, we can predict the trends and events that will unfold over a period of time.

The familiar kind of astrology that we see every day in newspapers and magazines is called Sun sign astrology. The Earth has a regular orbit around the Sun, and this makes the Sun appear against the background of each sign of the zodiac in turn, at set times of the year. This makes it easy for nonastrologers to figure out which sign they are born under.

Unfortunately, the Sun enters each sign at a different time, and sometimes even on a different day from one year to the next, which means that people born "on the cusp" (the point where one sign joins another sign) can find themselves described as belonging to the ending sign in some newspapers and magazines and the beginning sign in others. Astrologers use the exact degree for each individual, but newspapers have to use an average date, and they don't all settle on the same one. If you are not absolutely sure which Sun sign you come under, check with an astrologer.

YOUR SUN SIGN

The Sun is a life-giving force, and its position on your horoscope is bound to influence your personality, which, in turn, affects your potential for success, creativity, and happiness in various areas of life. The Sun is often associated with business, entertainment, and having a good time. It is also concerned with the children in your family. The Sun shows how you choose to spend your time and your money, and what you most enjoy. Other features on your birth chart will modify your Sun-sign nature, but it is usually apparent somewhere, and you will always have similarities with those who share your Sun sign.

THE MOON AND THE PLANETS

The Moon's position at your birth is almost as important as the position of your Sun sign. The Moon rules the emotional side of your nature, and its place in your birth chart reveals your underlying nature and motives. It is wise to check the elements and qualities of the Moon sign of any person you are likely to become deeply involved with—they may show you parts of that person that are quite different from what is being displayed on the outside.

Each planet rules a different aspect of a person's nature and of life—for example, a potentially flighty person can be anchored by Mars and Venus in earth signs, or a stodgy one can be lightened by Mercury, Venus, Mars, or Jupiter in air or fire signs. Fire signs show enthusiasm and impetuosity, earth signs denote practicality, air signs belong to ideas people, and water signs are intuitive and emotional.

Astrologers study many other features on a horoscope, both for character reading and also for prediction. These might include the midheaven, the descendant, the nadir, the asteroids, midpoints, fixed stars, the vertex, and much more, depending upon the skill of the astrologer and the nature of the work he wishes to do.

PREDICTION

There are a number of predictive techniques in astrology, but they all come down to checking the position of the planets at a specific time against their positions on the natal chart, to see what is happening and what is due to happen over a particular period of time.

THE WESTERN ZODIAC

The zodiac is the group of constellations that lie along the path that the Sun appears to take around the Earth.

THE SYMBOLS

Each sign of the zodiac is associated with a planet and a symbol. Every second sign (starting with Aries, then Gemini, etc.) is positive; the other signs are negative. Some astrologers express this concept with the words "masculine" and "feminine," or even "yang" and "yin," but the meaning is the same. Each sign also belongs to an

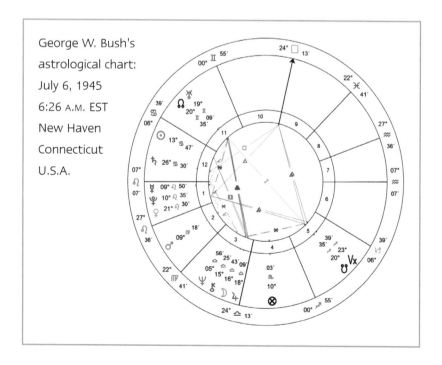

George W. Bush's astrological chart:
July 6, 1945
6:26 A.M. EST
New Haven
Connecticut
U.S.A.

element and a quality that give it a particular character. Your sign of the zodiac will have something in common with several others, but there are always four signs with which you don't share anything. However, you may have other factors in your individual chart that are not immediately apparent in a general description of your sign of the zodiac. Here are the signs of the zodiac with their basic features, so that you can see how this fits.

- Signs of the zodiac: Aries, Taurus, Gemini, Cancer, Leo, Virgo, Libra, Scorpio, Sagittarius, Capricorn, Aquarius, Pisces
- Positive, masculine, or yang signs have an extroverted, assertive, and quick-thinking nature. These are Aries, Gemini, Leo, Libra, Sagittarius, and Aquarius.
- Negative, feminine, or yin signs are introverted, slower to react, and more passive in nature. These signs are Taurus, Cancer, Virgo, Scorpio, Capricorn, and Pisces.
- The positive group splits again into the elements of fire and air. Fire signs are impulsive, enthusiastic, and quick to anger, but also quick to cool down. These are Aries, Leo, and Sagittarius. The air group is more intellectual, thoughtful, and inclined to fuss and worry. These signs are Gemini, Libra, and Aquarius.
- The negative group splits again into the elements of earth and water. Earth signs are practical, sensible, and disinclined to jump into new things. These are Taurus, Virgo, and Capricorn. The water group is sensitive and inclined to act from an emotional standpoint. These signs are Cancer, Scorpio, and Pisces.
- The signs are also grouped according to whether they are cardinal, fixed, or mutable. The cardinal signs are go-getters, the fixed signs uphold the status quo, and the mutable signs bring change and closure. The cardinal signs are Aries, Cancer, Libra, and Capricorn. The fixed signs are Taurus, Leo, Scorpio, and Aquarius, and the mutable signs are Gemini, Virgo, Sagittarius, and Pisces.

WESTERN RISING SIGNS

Your rising sign (also called your ascendant) is the sign that was crossing the eastern horizon when you were born. It is determined by the time of day, plus the date and place where you were born. It tells you about the influences that were around you during your childhood, and it modifies your Sun sign considerably. The sign opposite your rising sign is called your descendant, and it affects your choice of friends, lovers, colleagues, and partners.

During the course of each day, the Sun rises in one part of the world after another. Those with the same birthday share the same Sun sign, but they could have any one of the twelve signs rising up over the horizon, depending upon their time and place of birth.

The following method offers a rough guide to your rising sign. Find out what time the Sun rose on the day you were born, deducting one hour if daylight saving was in effect.

1 Look at the illustration. The time of day is arranged around the outside of the circle. It looks like a clock face, but it shows the whole twenty-four-hour day in two-hour blocks.

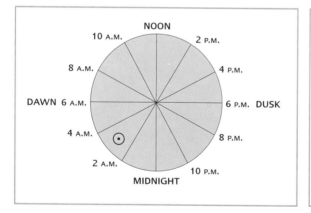

♈	Aries
♉	Taurus
♊	Gemini
♋	Cancer
♌	Leo
♍	Virgo
♎	Libra
♏	Scorpio
♐	Sagittarius
♑	Capricorn
♒	Aquarius
♓	Pisces

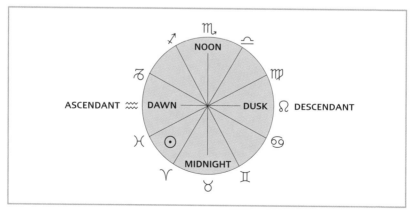

2 Write the astrological symbol that represents the Sun (a circle with a dot in the middle) in the area that corresponds to your time of birth.

3 Now write the name of your sign, or the symbol for your sign, on the line at the end of the block of time that your Sun falls into. Our example shows a person who was born between 2:00 A.M. and 4:00 A.M. under the sign of Pisces.

4 Write in either the names or the symbols of the zodiac signs in their correct order around the chart in a counterclockwise direction, starting with your own sign, as shown in the example.

5 The sign that appears on the left-hand side of the wheel at the "Dawn" line is your rising sign, or ascendant. The example shows a person born with the Sun in Pisces and with Aquarius rising. You will always find the ascendant sign on the "Dawn" line and the descendant sign on the "Dusk" line.

The rising sign relates to your early experiences of life and the things that influenced you in childhood. You may behave—and even look—more like your rising sign than your Sun sign. The following is a brief outline of the effects of the rising signs; the section on your Western Sun sign (in the "A–Z of Astrology" chapter) has extra information about the character of the sign that is rising.

Aries rising	Your outer manner is quiet and reserved.
Taurus rising	You have a calm outer manner, but with seething emotions beneath, and you may be possessive.
Gemini rising	You may be friendly and intelligent, but you often feel like an outsider.
Cancer rising	You have a responsible attitude and are good to your family.
Leo rising	You are attracted to glamorous situations and unusual people or careers.
Virgo rising	You are overly self-critical.
Libra rising	You are attractive and charming but can tend toward laziness.
Scorpio rising	You have poor relationships until you find the right lover.
Sagittarius rising	You need freedom and space.
Capricorn rising	You are cautious in love and with money.
Aquarius rising	You are intelligent and tend to be drawn to an unusual lifestyle.
Pisces rising	You are partly practical, businesslike, organized, careful with money, and partly spiritual, mystical, and chaotic.

Chinese Horoscopes

C hinese astrology provides useful insights into our individual characters, strengths, and weaknesses, and helps us understand how we relate to others. It is a method that accesses ancient Chinese wisdom and culture to determine the likely success and challenges in any of life's experiences—marriage, travel, having children, career, and health.

You need only a date and time of birth to be able to determine and analyze the following crucial elements of your Chinese astrology profile:

- The traits provided by the animals ruling the date and time of birth
- The energies present (yin or yang)
- The set of natural and dominant elements

The origins of Chinese astrology go back many thousands of years, and are steeped in ancient Chinese culture and philosophy. The ancient Chinese placed great importance on astrology, using it to shed light on individual personalities and make predictions for people about likely compatibilities before they plunged into business, marriage, friendship, and parenthood. The local astrologer was often an esteemed and trusted counselor, and his advice was taken seriously.

Chinese astrology was originally based on the movement of the seven stars of the Dipper, plus the Pole star and Vega, and on the cycles of the planets Jupiter and Saturn. Buddhist monks used astrology to make predictions for their followers. However, at one point a series of repressive emperors outlawed astrology. As they

were not allowed to use star names, the monks found other ways of incorporating the horoscope system into the calendar and numerology system that was already in use, and that was acceptable to the emperors—they developed the now-famous animal signs. These simplified the previous system and made it more accessible.

The names of the signs and elements vary a little from place to place; they also reflect the differences in nationality of the nineteenth-century Europeans, who translated the system into their own languages. Here are the main differences:

- Rat, Mouse
- Ox, Buffalo
- Rabbit, Hare, Cat
- Snake, Serpent
- Sheep, Goat
- Rooster, Cockerel, Hen, Chicken
- Pig, Boar
- Wood, Tree
- Earth, Soil
- Metal, Gold, Iron

The animal signs used in Chinese astrology, and their order, astrologically, have their basis in Buddhist legend. The legend says that when the great Buddha found enlightenment and was ready to leave the Earth, he invited all the land's creatures to his kingdom so that he could say farewell to them before his departure. Only twelve animals arrived, in this order: the Rat, the Ox, the Tiger, the Rabbit, the Dragon, the Snake, the Horse, the Sheep, the Monkey, the Rooster, the Dog, and finally the Pig.

The order in which the animals arrived at Buddha's side helps us understand some of their characters. The legend tells of a great river that all the animals had to cross just before reaching Buddha. The first to arrive at the river were the Rat and the Ox. The Rat immediately saw that he needed the Ox's assistance to cross the raging river and asked the Ox for a lift on his back. The Ox agreed. On reaching the other side, the smart-thinking Rat sprang from the Ox's back and raced up the riverbank so that he would be the first to arrive and, therefore, the first to be honored by Buddha. The hardworking Ox came in second.

ORDER	ANIMAL	MOTTO	ORDER	ANIMAL	MOTTO
1	Rat	"I think"	7	Horse	"I run free"
2	Ox	"Patient"	8	Sheep	"I adapt"
3	Tiger	"Courage"	9	Monkey	"I entertain"
4	Rabbit	"Discreet"	10	Rooster	"Resilient"
5	Dragon	"Majestic"	11	Dog	"I am loyal"
6	Snake	"I sense"	12	Pig	"I am eager"

To thank the animals for answering his call, Buddha decided to celebrate each of them. Their reward was that each New Year would be celebrated in their honor. Accordingly, in every twelve-year cycle, each of the twelve animals is celebrated in turn. This means that people born during a specific year will be influenced, in terms of personality and life events, by the animal that the year celebrates.

THE FULL SYSTEM

The full Chinese astrology system is called "the Four Pillars" or "the Four Emperors." It incorporates animal signs, elements, yang and yin, and the *I Ching*. It relies upon the time, place, day, month, and year of birth, and it is extremely complex. This system requires the use of a special logbook called the "Universal or Perpetual Calendar." It is only available in Chinese, having never been properly translated into English.

One way of working with Chinese astrology is to start with the animal sign governing your year of birth—look up the Chinese Year Chart on pages 19–21 to see which it is. This is your dominant sign. You can then figure out your animal sign for the month of your birth. The traits of the animal ruling the month you were born in provide a more detailed analysis of your personality in intimate relationships (see the table on page 18). Next, figure out your hourly animal sign (see the table on page 18). This is your ascendant

animal sign, and it will tell you about your secret self. The traits of the animal sign governing your year of birth will describe your personality. This is the personality that others see—the one you show to the world. However, this can be moderated by the traits of the animals ruling your month and time of birth.

Figuring out your yearly animal sign

Each of the twelve animals of Chinese astrology has distinct personality traits associated with it. These traits are transferred to those born in the year governed by that animal.

Ruling year of birth = Dominant sign

Unlike the Western system, which records time in solar years—a solar year is the Earth's 365-day rotation around the Sun—the Chinese system measures time in lunar years, which follow the Moon's orbit around the Earth. The Chinese New Year falls on a different date every year, but always in January or February. If you were born during these months, consult the Chinese Year Chart to find out which animal dominates the year you were born in.

Figuring out your monthly animal sign

The Chinese monthly system starts the year with the month of February, which is around the time of the Chinese New Year. The original system would have run from February 4, which is the "imperial" New Year's Day, with each month starting on the fourth, but modern astrologers usually work from the first of each month.

Ruling month of birth = Love sign

The traits of the animal sign governing your month of birth (see the table on page 18) will reveal your character in intimate relationships. Knowing these traits will help you create a more detailed profile of yourself, which will, in turn, enable you to find a compatible partner in any intimate situation.

Figuring out your hourly animal sign

The animal sign ruling over the time of your birth is your ascendant sign. Like the element that governs your year (see pages 22–23), your ascendant sign modifies the characteristics of your dominant sign. The ascendant sign indicates your hidden self. This is the way you perceive yourself; it is the side you will conceal from others.

The ancient Chinese broke the day into two-hour segments, each of which is ruled by one of the animal signs; if you know what time you were born, you can find out which is your hourly sign from the table below. If you were born during daylight saving, deduct one hour from your time of birth. If you are not sure which of two signs you come under, read both.

MONTH	ANIMAL
December	Rat
January	Ox
February	Tiger
March	Rabbit
April	Dragon
May	Snake
June	Horse
July	Sheep
August	Monkey
September	Rooster
October	Dog
November	Pig

THE HOUR	ANIMAL
11:00 P.M. to 1:00 A.M.	Rat
1:00 A.M. to 3:00 A.M.	Ox
3:00 A.M. to 5:00 A.M.	Tiger
5:00 A.M. to 7:00 A.M.	Rabbit
7:00 A.M. to 9:00 A.M.	Dragon
9:00 A.M. to 11:00 A.M.	Snake
11:00 A.M. to 1:00 P.M.	Horse
1:00 P.M. to 3:00 P.M.	Sheep
3:00 P.M. to 5:00 P.M.	Monkey
5:00 P.M. to 7:00 P.M.	Rooster
7:00 P.M. to 9:00 P.M.	Dog
9:00 P.M. to 11:00 P.M.	Pig

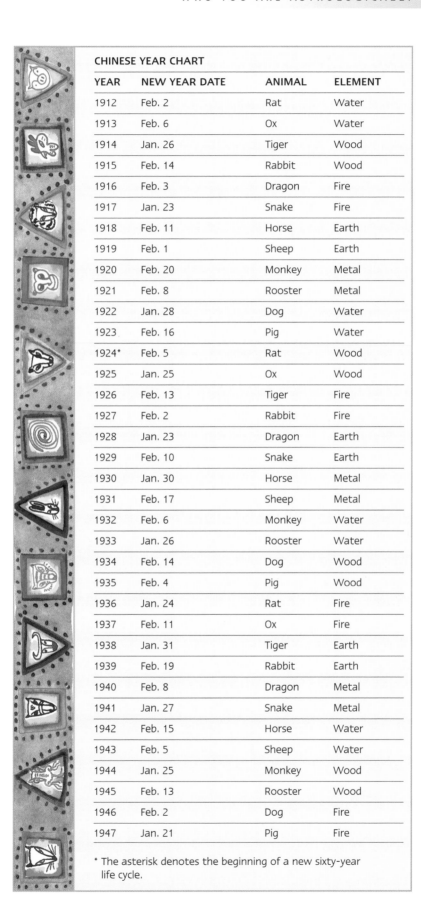

CHINESE YEAR CHART

YEAR	NEW YEAR DATE	ANIMAL	ELEMENT
1912	Feb. 2	Rat	Water
1913	Feb. 6	Ox	Water
1914	Jan. 26	Tiger	Wood
1915	Feb. 14	Rabbit	Wood
1916	Feb. 3	Dragon	Fire
1917	Jan. 23	Snake	Fire
1918	Feb. 11	Horse	Earth
1919	Feb. 1	Sheep	Earth
1920	Feb. 20	Monkey	Metal
1921	Feb. 8	Rooster	Metal
1922	Jan. 28	Dog	Water
1923	Feb. 16	Pig	Water
1924*	Feb. 5	Rat	Wood
1925	Jan. 25	Ox	Wood
1926	Feb. 13	Tiger	Fire
1927	Feb. 2	Rabbit	Fire
1928	Jan. 23	Dragon	Earth
1929	Feb. 10	Snake	Earth
1930	Jan. 30	Horse	Metal
1931	Feb. 17	Sheep	Metal
1932	Feb. 6	Monkey	Water
1933	Jan. 26	Rooster	Water
1934	Feb. 14	Dog	Wood
1935	Feb. 4	Pig	Wood
1936	Jan. 24	Rat	Fire
1937	Feb. 11	Ox	Fire
1938	Jan. 31	Tiger	Earth
1939	Feb. 19	Rabbit	Earth
1940	Feb. 8	Dragon	Metal
1941	Jan. 27	Snake	Metal
1942	Feb. 15	Horse	Water
1943	Feb. 5	Sheep	Water
1944	Jan. 25	Monkey	Wood
1945	Feb. 13	Rooster	Wood
1946	Feb. 2	Dog	Fire
1947	Jan. 21	Pig	Fire

* The asterisk denotes the beginning of a new sixty-year life cycle.

YEAR	NEW YEAR DATE	ANIMAL	ELEMENT
1948	Feb. 10	Rat	Earth
1949	Jan. 29	Ox	Earth
1950	Feb. 17	Tiger	Metal
1951	Feb. 6	Rabbit	Metal
1952	Jan. 27	Dragon	Water
1953	Feb. 14	Snake	Water
1954	Feb. 3	Horse	Wood
1955	Jan. 24	Sheep	Wood
1956	Feb. 12	Monkey	Fire
1957	Jan. 31	Rooster	Fire
1958	Feb. 18	Dog	Earth
1959	Feb. 8	Pig	Earth
1960	Jan. 28	Rat	Metal
1961	Feb. 15	Ox	Metal
1962	Feb. 5	Tiger	Water
1963	Jan. 25	Rabbit	Water
1964	Feb. 13	Dragon	Wood
1965	Feb. 2	Snake	Wood
1966	Jan. 21	Horse	Fire
1967	Feb. 9	Sheep	Fire
1968	Jan. 30	Monkey	Earth
1969	Feb. 17	Rooster	Earth
1970	Feb. 6	Dog	Metal
1971	Jan. 27	Pig	Metal
1972	Jan. 16	Rat	Water
1973	Feb. 3	Ox	Water
1974	Jan. 23	Tiger	Wood
1975	Feb. 11	Rabbit	Wood
1976	Jan. 31	Dragon	Fire
1977	Feb. 18	Snake	Fire
1978	Feb. 7	Horse	Earth
1979	Jan. 28	Sheep	Earth
1980	Feb. 16	Monkey	Metal
1981	Feb. 5	Rooster	Metal
1982	Jan. 25	Dog	Water
1983	Feb. 13	Pig	Water
1984*	Feb. 2	Rat	Wood

* The asterisk denotes the beginning of a new sixty-year life cycle. The year 1984 starts the 78th Chinese life cycle.

YEAR	NEW YEAR DATE	ANIMAL	ELEMENT
1985	Feb. 20	Ox	Wood
1986	Feb. 9	Tiger	Fire
1987	Jan. 30	Rabbit	Fire
1988	Feb. 17	Dragon	Earth
1989	Feb. 6	Snake	Earth
1990	Jan. 27	Horse	Metal
1991	Feb. 15	Sheep	Metal
1992	Feb. 4	Monkey	Water
1993	Jan. 23	Rooster	Water
1994	Feb. 10	Dog	Wood
1995	Jan. 31	Pig	Wood
1996	Feb. 19	Rat	Fire
1997	Feb. 8	Ox	Fire
1998	Jan. 28	Tiger	Earth
1999	Feb. 16	Rabbit	Earth
2000	Feb. 5	Dragon	Metal
2001	Jan. 24	Snake	Metal
2002	Feb. 12	Horse	Water
2003	Feb. 1	Sheep	Water
2004	Jan. 22	Monkey	Wood
2005	Feb. 9	Rooster	Wood
2006	Jan. 29	Dog	Fire
2007	Feb. 18	Pig	Fire
2008	Feb. 7	Rat	Earth
2009	Jan. 26	Ox	Earth
2010	Feb. 14	Tiger	Metal
2011	Feb. 3	Rabbit	Metal
2012	Jan. 23	Dragon	Water
2013	Feb. 10	Snake	Water
2014	Jan. 31	Horse	Wood
2015	Feb. 19	Sheep	Wood
2016	Feb. 8	Monkey	Fire
2017	Jan. 28	Rooster	Fire
2018	Feb. 16	Dog	Earth
2019	Feb. 5	Pig	Earth

YOUR RULING ELEMENTS

Life is said to revolve around the dynamic interaction of the five earthly elements—wood, fire, earth, metal, and water. Just like each of the twelve animals of the Chinese zodiac, each element is associated with specific character traits. Wood is idealistic, fire is intellectual and enthusiastic, earth is practical, metal is determined and stubborn, and water is artistic, communicative, and businesslike.

Each animal sign has a natural element that influences its core traits. In addition, each animal is also influenced by the element governing its year—this provides five distinct personality types within each animal group (see Chinese Year Chart on pages 19–21). The element governing the year of birth is the dominant element.

The dominant element's influence on each animal results in five distinct personality types for each animal. Hence there is, in

---

EXAMPLE OF A PERSON'S PERSONALITY PROFILE

according to Chinese astrology

EXAMPLE: Steve • *Date of Birth:* 11/29/63 • *Time:* 8:30 A.M.

DOMINANT SIGN AND ELEMENT: Water Rabbit

   Element: Wood • *Energy:* Yin

ASCENDANT SIGN: Dragon (Note: based on time of birth)

   Element: Earth • *Energy:* Yang

LOVE SIGN: Pig (Note: based on month of birth)

   Element: Water • *Energy:* Yin

ENERGIES: Yin ~ Yang ~ Yin

Steve's profile shows a good balance between yin and yang energies. His personality is neither introverted nor extroverted, but he has a preference for introversion.

Animal signs: Rabbit ~ Dragon ~ Pig • The mix of animal signs ensures that Steve has a comprehensive array of character traits. The Dragon ascendant assures that he has strength and willpower when they are needed.

Elements: Wood ~ Earth ~ Water • Steve's mix of elements is positive, harmonious, and centered on the softer, more creative elements—wood and water. As there is no fire or metal present, Steve is quite easygoing and artistic, but he has a practical, realistic mindset (influence of the earth element).

ELEMENT	COLOR	CHARACTERISTICS
Wood	Green	Growth, solid, stable, dependable
Fire	Red	Vibrant, wild, passionate, unpredictable
Earth	Yellow	Grounded, balanced, nurturing, wise
Metal	White	Useful, ambitious, tenacious, strong
Water	Black	Mysterious, communicative, intuitive, flexible

Chinese astrology, the potential for sixty (twelve animals times five elements) identifiable personalities. For example, a Water Tiger would be much more easygoing and temperate than its Metal Tiger sibling, who could be quite fiery and volatile.

The elements governing years of birth

METAL *See pages 82–84:*
1900, 1901, 1910, 1911, 1920, 1921, 1930, 1931, 1940, 1941, 1950, 1951, 1960, 1961, 1970, 1971, 1980, 1981, 1990, 1991, 2000, 2001, 2010, 2011

WATER *See pages 84–85:*
1902, 1903, 1912, 1913, 1922, 1923, 1932, 1933, 1942, 1943, 1952, 1953, 1962, 1963, 1972, 1973, 1982, 1983, 1992, 1993, 2002, 2003, 2012, 2013

WOOD *See pages 86–87:*
1904, 1905, 1914, 1915, 1924, 1925, 1934, 1935, 1944, 1945, 1954, 1955, 1964, 1965, 1974, 1975, 1984, 1985, 1994, 1995, 2004, 2005, 2014, 2015

FIRE *See pages 80–82:*
1916, 1917, 1926, 1927, 1936, 1937, 1946, 1947, 1956, 1957, 1966, 1967, 1976, 1977, 1986, 1987, 1996, 1997, 2006, 2007, 2016, 2017

EARTH *See pages 78–80:*
1918, 1919, 1928, 1929, 1938, 1939, 1948, 1949, 1958, 1959, 1968, 1969, 1978, 1979, 1988, 1989, 1998, 1999, 2008, 2009, 2018, 2019

Following the Ganzhi Lunar Calendar, the Chinese record time in sixty-year cycles. They believe that a full life is lived over a sixty-year period. Hence the 60th birthday is widely celebrated in China, as it is seen as the point at which wisdom is achieved. This ensures that each element governs and influences each animal sign only once during a life cycle. For example, Water Rats were born in the lunar years of 1912 and 1972—a span of sixty years.

Combining East and West

By combining the traits of your Chinese and Western zodiac signs, you can obtain a more detailed profile of your character; this could identify unique subtleties that may help you understand your communication style and improve your chances of success in relationships and careers.

While the Chinese and Western astrology systems differ, there are some key similarities. Each system:

- has twelve core signs, often represented by an animal;
- divides the twelve signs into four groups of three, to highlight compatibility; and
- relies on elements (earth, fire, water, etc.) to reveal the differences between members of each animal sign and commonalities between signs.

Here are some of the fundamental differences:

THE CHINESE SYSTEM

This is based on a sixty-year life cycle, within which one of the twelve animal signs, matched every year with one of the five elements, rules for a whole lunar year:

12 signs x 5 elements = 60

Each animal sign has both a primary and a dominant element influencing its traits.

THE WESTERN ZODIAC

This zodiac does not have a "life cycle"; the system is a continuum. It is based on the solar year, where each sign rules for approximately thirty days of the 365-day year. Each sign is associated with only one primary element, of which there are four.

Elements of the Western zodiac

ELEMENT	CHARACTERISTICS
Fire	Passionate, energetic, courageous, wild, vibrant, unpredictable
Air	Intelligent, wise, thoughtful, analytical, cautious, detached
Earth	Grounded, practical, balanced, realistic, materialistic
Water	Emotional, intuitive, considerate, generous, flexible

Signs of the Western zodiac

SIGN	DATES	ELEMENT	ENERGY
Aries: the Ram	Mar. 21–Apr. 19	Fire	Masculine/positive
Taurus: the Bull	Apr. 20–May 20	Earth	Feminine/negative
Gemini: the Twins	May 21–Jun. 20	Air	Masculine/positive
Cancer: the Crab	Jun. 21–Jul. 22	Water	Feminine/negative
Leo: the Lion	Jul. 23–Aug. 22	Fire	Masculine/positive
Virgo: the Virgin	Aug. 23–Sep. 22	Earth	Feminine/negative
Libra: the Scales	Sep. 23–Oct. 22	Air	Masculine/positive
Scorpio: the Scorpion	Oct. 23–Nov. 21	Water	Feminine/negative
Sagittarius: the Archer	Nov. 22–Dec. 21	Fire	Masculine/positive
Capricorn: the Goat	Dec. 22–Jan. 19	Earth	Feminine/negative
Aquarius: the Water Carrier	Jan. 20–Feb.18	Air	Masculine/positive
Pisces: the Fish	Feb. 19–Mar. 20	Water	Feminine/negative

Compatibility groups

Fire signs	Aries/Leo/Sagittarius
Air signs	Gemini/Libra/Aquarius
Earth signs	Taurus/Virgo/Capricorn
Water signs	Cancer/Scorpio/Pisces

Character traits for Western zodiac signs

SIGN	CHARACTER TRAITS
Aries	Competitive, energetic, enthusiastic, impulsive, daring
Taurus	Patient, logical, tenacious, determined, sensuous
Gemini	Intelligent, articulate, witty, ingenious, perceptive
Cancer	Affectionate, considerate, cautious, emotional, imaginative
Leo	Loyal, powerful, noble, dynamic, charismatic, brave
Virgo	Refined, practical, proper, gentle, particular, gracious
Libra	Balanced, charming, intelligent, idealistic, fair
Scorpio	Reserved, mysterious, sensitive, alluring, calculating
Sagittarius	Free-spirited, open, friendly, physical, adventurous
Capricorn	Ambitious, hardworking, dependable, tenacious
Aquarius	Idealistic, innovative, individual, visionary, spiritual
Pisces	Creative, sensitive, emotional, intuitive, flexible

How to combine the two systems

1 Add your Western sign traits and the associated element characteristics to those of your dominant Chinese animal sign.

2 Note the energy type of both your Chinese animal (yin or yang) and your Western sign (masculine or feminine).

3 Look for similarities and contrasts among all the traits. Are specific traits heightened as a result, or are they more varied?

4 Determine whether or not a balance is achieved between the two types of energies.

Chinese	Western
Yang =	masculine/positive
Yin =	feminine/negative

5 Do the elements vary, or does one dominate? How do the elements' characteristics influence your animal traits?

As the Chinese say, the purpose of astrology is to achieve balance and harmony through knowing better both your character and the characters of others.

AN EXAMPLE

Oprah Winfrey, talk show host
(b. January 29, 1954)

Profile	Sign	Elements	Energy
Chinese:	Snake	Natural: fire	Yin
		Dominant: water	
Western:	Aquarius	Air	Masculine/positive

Summary of combined profiles The energy is ideally balanced in this combined profile. There is a display of traits with a balance of elements, with the emphasis on intellectual and intuitive ability coming from the traits of both signs. Aquarian Snakes are ruled by their minds; they are deep and original thinkers who are skilled at sensing the mood in any situation and are able to respond appropriately. Both Snakes and Aquarians like to take a detached, almost voyeuristic, approach to life.

Animal Totem Astrology

The Native Americans are a diverse group of peoples. The Americas represent a large segment of the world's landmass, and Native Americans have for centuries lived everywhere from the frozen north to as far south as the tropical jungles. Their religious beliefs and practices vary widely. Some started out with a basis in astronomy and astrology, while others used geomancy, which is the study of landmarks, the marks of animals, and other indications on the surface of the land.

The earliest forms of star-based astrology systems were Toltec and Mayan; these systems were later taken up by the Aztecs and, over time, some of this thinking moved northward. Nowadays, the mythology and astrology of the various Native American peoples have crystallized into a popular form of astrology.

Native Americans believe in personal communication with the Creator Spirit, and they receive most of their information through visions, often with the aid of a medicine man who is part healer and part clairvoyant. Native Americans also believe in the Earth Mother, who looks after the land, and they try to live in harmony with nature. Along the way, a study of the stars became incorporated into these beliefs. Some peoples would view an area of land several miles in diameter as an exact copy of one or more of the constellations.

They also believe that all life on the earth, in the water world, and in the sky and heavens has a spiritual essence. All animals, plants, or minerals in these worlds have a spiritual core, a unique and intangible power. And all living things collectively form one Great Spirit—the spirit of all life. They also believe that animals, fish, and birds hold great power—power to communicate messages between the natural and the spiritual worlds.

Native Americans believe the purpose of life for each individual is to find and keep to a particular spiritual path. This can only be achieved by living each day in conscious awareness of your thoughts, words, and deeds. Native Americans believe true harmony in life comes from appreciating and paying homage to everything on the earth, in the water, and in the skies.

Native Americans draw many parallels between the elements of earth, air, fire, and water, the seasons, and aspects of human personality. These parallels provide specific guidelines for maintaining optimal physical, emotional, and psychological health and for the medicine required if disease occurs. Their knowledge of nature and the seasons also enables Native Americans to make prophecies for the future of their people as a whole.

In Native American tribal life, wise men, called shamans, have always been held in special reverence. Shamans are believed to have the power to recognize the intricate relationship between the natural and supernatural worlds, and to draw conclusions for the person or group involved.

For instance, by looking at each seasonal period and the particular animals, colors, stones, and plants that have an affinity with that period, shamans can accurately describe people's character and purpose in life. This information can then be used as powerful medicine for individuals who are looking for advice on current troubles, and for supporting people on their life's journey.

THE BASICS OF ANIMAL TOTEM ASTROLOGY

Native Americans drew many parallels between nature and the seasons and the elements of human personality. They believed that the season in which you were born influenced your personality.

Animal totem astrology, as practiced by Native Americans in the past and today, is a system that associates a particular totem, which is an animal, fish, or bird, with a particular time of birth, season of birth, or element of nature. Each of the twelve signs also belongs to a clan that shares its element—Thunderbird for fire, Turtle for earth, Butterfly for air, and Frog for water.

As with most systems, there are also variations—different peoples in the vast territory of the Americas have differing totems for time of birth, the seasons, and/or the elements. This dictionary presents the most common and widely known of the animal totems.

You will find the animal totem astrological system both relevant and useful no matter where in the world you were born or where you are living today. The totems and affinities still hold their power regardless of your distance from the natural home of the Native Americans. Knowing your totem animal and the nature of the other totem animals will help you:

• understand your own personality as well as your relationship with others, nature, and the earth and its seasons;
• answer your questions about the path you are meant to travel in your life;
• identify the totems and affinities that will support you and help you stay balanced, and that offer protection from harm; and
• build rapport and maintain harmonious relationships with others.

Knowing your animal totem can give you insight into your own nature. In times of trouble, associating yourself with the animal totems of other people will allow you to take on the characteristics of others and understand more about yourself. The twelve animal totems are: Snow Goose, Otter, Wolf, Hawk, Beaver, Deer, Woodpecker, Salmon, Brown Bear, Raven, Snake, and Owl. Details of each of these animal totems is explored in the A–Z section of this book.

In the belief system of Native Americans, each animal totem is not complete unto itself; each relies on the others for wholeness and balance. Some totems complement others; some have an active energy flow, others a receptive energy flow, for example. This means that some signs are more introspective, others more outward looking.

Apart from unique gifts and attributes, each animal totem also brings specific challenges to those born during its time. The attributes, gifts, traits, and challenges combine to outline each individual's purpose in life.

THE MEDICINE WHEEL

The Medicine Wheel is part compass and part wheel of fortune, and it moves through the seasons, through lifetimes, and through good times and bad. The full Medicine Wheel is a large, round, pictorial almanac that shows the movement of the seasons, planets, and constellations during the course of the year. All cultures use wheels and circles to denote the passage of the stars around the Earth, and thus the passage of time, seasons, and the events of our lives.

Somewhere along the line, Native Americans moved from a lunar calendar to a Western calendar, so their totem signs now fit reasonably comfortably with our familiar Western ones. One difference is that the cycle starts at the solstice that occurs just before Christmas, rather than the equinox on March 21.

The Native Americans associate each season with a compass point. North is winter, cold and dark, the time when the earth rests; the east brings dawning, awakening, and the spring; the south represents the height of summer and the start of the harvest; and the west is the area of strong winds, cooler weather, and a time for hunting—or for war. Each season has a Spirit Keeper attached to it.

The table opposite lists the core elements of the traditional Medicine Wheel.

A note on the compass directions: They represent affinities with elements of life. North represents darkness and is hence associated with winter, whereas south represents light and is hence associated with summer, a time of long days. Animal totems with the direction north—the winter totems—would be those with a more introspective, spiritual nature, as the coldness of the winter season would cause people to spend more time indoors and less time engaged in physical activities in the world outside.

Note also that the *S* at the center of the Medicine Wheel (see page 114) represents the never-ending flow of energy, the life force.

The shamans use symbolic ornaments and totems to help individuals understand themselves and others. They have integrated all the seasonal birth times with their symbolic ornaments and totems in the Medicine Wheel. Using the Wheel, shamans demonstrate how harmony and balance among all elements of life on earth can be achieved. They can also show how everything has its place in tribal life and in the world of the land, seas, and skies as a whole. Ill fortune will come if the balance is disrupted.

Each of the twelve birth times also provides distinct gifts and talents that a shaman can use to heal the troubles of his people. For example, people born during the dead of winter, that is, the cleansing time, are closely connected to the life spirit—they have prophetic powers and, at the very least, latent healing powers. A person in pain, either physically or spiritually, would be advised to spend time with someone born during the cleansing period. Also, at times when it is necessary to look ahead to the future to seek answers to present dilemmas, the tribal shaman will call on the totems and affinities of the cleansing period for assistance.

See also the entry for Medicine Wheel on pages 114–115.

TIME OF THE YEAR	ANIMAL TOTEM	ELEMENT
Renewal	Snow Goose	Earth
Cleansing	Otter	Air
Strong winds	Wolf	Water
Budding	Hawk	Fire
Growing	Beaver	Earth
Flowering	Deer	Air
Long days	Woodpecker	Water
Ripening	Salmon	Fire
Harvesting	Brown Bear	Earth
Falling leaves	Raven	Air
Frosting	Snake	Water
Long nights	Owl	Fire

OTHER ANCIENT SYSTEMS

Arabic Astrology

The Arabs developed a form of astrology that is based on a circular chart and planets in much the same way that Western astrology is, but which then takes a completely different approach. This form of astrology is known to Western astrologers as the Arabic Parts, and in the Middle East as the Fortunes of Astrology.

Various Arabic astrologers worked on these fortunes. There are twenty-four fortunes that can be calculated for any individual. They each have a specific purpose and cover a particular aspect of a person's life. In 1029, an astrologer named Al-Biruni compiled a comprehensive list of the twenty-four

fortunes—what they mean and how to calculate them. His book was only updated and properly translated into English in 1980, by an American astrologer named Robert Hurzt Granite.

One of the most famous fortunes used in Arabic astrology is called the Part of Fortune. Also known as the Part of the Moon, it is the only fortune in common use by Western astrologers. The Part of Fortune shows how a person will make headway in life—how they will prosper materially and emotionally.

The starting point for the calculation of each fortune is the exact degree of a person's rising sign at the time of their birth. This exact degree is known as the ascendant. After this, a series of formulas must be worked through to find each fortune.

To calculate the Part of Fortune for a daytime birth, add the position of the Moon to the position of the ascendant, then subtract the number of degrees between the Sun and Moon from the first figure:

Ascendant + Moon - Sun

This formula reverses for night births: The Moon's position is subtracted from the ascendant, then the distance between the Moon and the Sun is calculated and added to the first number. The formula for the Part of Fortune for a nighttime birth is below:

Ascendant - Moon + Sun

Calculations for other fortunes are even more complicated, as they involve the ascendant, two planets, and the cusp of a particular astrological house. Some formulas are the same for day and night, but others are not. This kind of astrology requires a top-notch astrologer who either can handle the calculations with ease or has software that can do the job.

There are many of these fortunes or Arabic parts, with names such as the Part of Goods, the Part of Brethren, the Part of Servants, the Part of Passion, the Part of Water Journeys, the Part of Imprisonment, the Part of Deception, and so on. Together, these fortunes provide guidance on every aspect of Arabic life.

Vedic Astrology

Vedic astrology is practiced in India, Sri Lanka, and surrounding areas. It takes seven years to gain a degree in Vedic astrology in a good school in India. A knowledgeable Western astrologer can read a basic Vedic chart because the differences are not great, but beyond the basics, the two systems diverge. Vedic charts are usually square in shape, although some Indian astrologers also use round charts similar to those used in the West.

One glaring difference is that Western astrologers use the tropical zodiac while Vedic astrologers use the sidereal (star) zodiac. The tropical zodiac starts at the spring equinox in the Northern Hemisphere, on March 21. This becomes the start of the sign of Aries; the rest of the signs follow, from Taurus through to Pisces.

Vedic astrology is based on the constellations rather than the equinoxes, so it uses sidereal time rather than earth or calendar time. The constellations on which Vedic astrology is based have moved since the rules of Western astrology were originally laid down around 2,000 years ago—they have precessed backward through the zodiac. In Western astrology before the Christian era, the Earth was moving through the sign of Taurus to Aries, and entered the sign of Pisces at the start of the Christian era. We are now on the cusp of the sign of Aquarius.

The rules for Vedic astrology, however, were laid down after the time of Christ, which means that if you were born in the Western sign of Libra, by Vedic astrology you would now be a Virgo. If you construct a Vedic chart for a time several hundred years in the future, your Sun sign would shift even further back, into Leo.

Vedic astrologers don't concentrate on the signs of the zodiac in the way Western astrologers do. Vedic astrology is more complicated, taking into account the exact degree of each planet's position in the sky and many different ways of dividing and interpreting a chart—explaining this in detail is beyond the scope of this book.

Modern Vedic astrology uses all ten planets, though some systems revert to the older form, which only uses the seven planets that people can see with the naked eye. The seven planets are the

Sun, the Moon, Mercury, Venus, Mars, Jupiter, and Saturn. The later discoveries—Uranus, Neptune, and Pluto—were eventually incorporated into both the Western and Vedic astrological systems.

Vedic astrology is frequently used for predictive purposes, such as plotting the best time to start an enterprise or the best date for a marriage. One common form of character reading is for an astrologer to assess a child's potential for a future career through the details of his or her chart.

One major difference between Western and Vedic astrology is the use of a system called Nakshatras. This type of astrology is also called the Mansions of the Moon. The Mansions system turns up in some forms of Arabic astrology, in Chinese astrology, and in some ancient Romany types of astrology. It predates our type of zodiac astrology by several centuries, though it is no longer used in Western astrology.

There are twenty-seven mansions, each one named after a deity or traditional being. Each is a segment of a circle—a 13°20' segment, to be exact. The first mansion starts from the beginning of the sidereal sign of Aries, which by our Western calendar starts around February 25. Once these mansions have been worked out, the Vedic astrologer inspects each one to see which planets are sitting in it and then examines the impact of those planets on the life and personality of the client. (The Arab and Chinese systems use twenty-eight divisions rather than twenty-seven.)

Rough dates for these mansions have been worked out. Simply look up the month of your birth in this dictionary and you can read about what each mansion can tell you about your personality. This is a rough guide—if your birthday falls close to the cusp (the point where two signs join) of two mansions, read both mansions.

WESTERN ZODIAC NAMES AND EQUIVALENT VEDIC ZODIAC NAMES

Note: Dates between Western and Vedic zodiac are not the same

Aries	Mesha	Libra	Thula
Taurus	Vrishaba	Scorpio	Vrishchika
Gemini	Mithuna	Sagittarius	Dhanus
Cancer	Karkarta	Capricorn	Makara
Leo	Simha	Aquarius	Kumbha
Virgo	Kanya	Pisces	Meena

Mayan and Aztec Astrology

The Mayans developed an early calendar, called the Solar Calendar, which contained eighteen lunar months, each of twenty days' duration, with an additional five-day month tacked on at the end of the year for a total of 365 days. According to some, the Mayan calendar predicts that the world is due to come to an end in the year 2012!

The Aztecs conquered the Mayans, but they also learned from them, adopting the Mayan Solar Calendar for agriculture. The Aztecs also developed their own calendar, called the Count of the Destinies, or the Destiny Calendar, which ran for 260 days. It was linked to various astronomical phenomena and was used for religious and ritual purposes, as well as for divination. Their divination was not the personal kind that we are familiar with; it was used to predict floods, harvests, drought, or war with neighboring nations.

The Aztecs believed that the universe was controlled by gods whose powers shifted from one to another in a very delicate balance. This power was either reflected in the stars or kept in place by them, so any change in the cosmos was likely to lead to

destruction of the Earth. In the Destiny Calendar, each segment of time was assigned to a god, and rituals were designed to keep these gods happy— one ritual, now very well known, was the sacrifice of preadolescent children.

The Destiny Calendar consists of two continuous sequences, which can be imagined as two interlocking wheels, the first with thirteen numbers, the second with twenty symbols. Start the cycle with the number 1 on the first wheel and the first symbol on the second wheel, with the thirteen numbers running in sequence then continually repeating, and the twenty signs doing the same. The first number and the first symbol will thus match up every 260 days (thirteen times twenty).

There are two different Destiny Calendars, and they were used for different purposes: one was for religious life, the other for general life. The Solar Calendar rotates in a fifty-two-year cycle vaguely reminiscent of the Chinese system—twelve signs that each rule one year and five elements that rule two years at a time, forming a repeating cycle. When the 260-day Destiny Calendar and the 365-day Solar Calendar start on the same day, it then takes roughly fifty-two years for them to reach their beginning dates on the same day again.

In the Aztec use of the Solar Calendar, each of the fifty-two years has a name. There are also thirteen-year eras that repeat the year names. The first of these is called Calli (one), the second, Tochtli (two), and so on. After fifty-two years (four times thirteen), the era name and the year name are the same.

As if this is not confusing enough, each of the twenty symbols in the Destiny Calendar is assigned to a specific god, but some are also assigned to the thirteen Destiny Calendar numbers. Remember, we are dealing with a Solar Calendar of fifty-two years, as well as a Destiny Calendar that comprises two cycles, one with twenty days and another with thirteen days. Therefore, one day might be expressed as:

---

18 Tecpatl Chalchihuitotolin - 9 Atl Xiuhtechuhtli

In this case, the first name represents god number 18 on the Destiny Calendar and day number 9 on the Solar Calendar, but either name could turn up in other places on either calendar.

Virtually every Central American civilization until the Spanish conquest adopted the Solar Calendar and the Destiny Calendar. The names varied from culture to culture, but the system was the same. The Solar Calendar is still used today in some parts of Mexico.

One survivor of the Destiny Calendar is the name of the Aztec god of violent and sudden change, which is Huracan—the root of the word "hurricane."

Mayan and Aztec astrology were never used for personal character reading or personal predictions.

Celtic Astrology

Trees figured strongly in pagan mythology all over northern Europe, and they were often worshiped, as different types of trees were associated with various ancient gods. The idea of bringing a Christmas tree into the house was encouraged by Queen Victoria's German husband, Prince Albert; it provided a direct link to the earlier pagan beliefs that surround the winter solstice.

It is likely that the idea of judging a person's nature and destiny by their type of Celtic tree comes from an ancient system that blended with an early form of solar and lunar astrology. The Celtic tree system contains forty-four signs, each of which has its own character. Most signs cover only a few days; the signs for the equinoxes and solstices each have only one day. These one-day signs were attached to pagan rituals that were performed at the turn of each season.

There are twenty-three trees associated with the signs, so some trees rule more than one segment of the year, but differences in temperament are detailed for those born under the same tree signs during different seasons. It would be nice and neat if the Fir tree ruled the Christmas period, but according to Celtic astrology, it is the Apple that rules the winter solstice.

The trees in this system seem to come from all over Europe and the Middle East; it is possible that the system arose in the Celtic areas of northwest Europe and traveled out and then back again, absorbing ideas from other parts of the continent.

If you look up your birth month in the "A–Z of Astrology" section of this book you can read about what your tree can tell you about your personality.

CELTIC TREES	PERIOD OF INFLUENCE
Fir	January 2–January 11
Elm	January 12–January 24
Cypress	January 25–February 3
Poplar	February 4–February 8
Cedar	February 9–February 18
Pine	February 19–March 10
Lime	March 11–March 20
Oak	March 21
Hazel	March 22–April 10
Maple	April 11–April 20
Walnut	April 21–May 14
Sweet Chestnut	May 15–May 24
Mountain Ash	May 25–June 3
Hornbeam	June 4–June 13
Fig	June 14–June 23
Birch	June 24
Apple	June 25–July 3
Fir	July 4–July 14
Elm	July 15–July 25
Cypress	July 26–August 4
Poplar	August 5–August 13
Cedar	August 14–August 23
Pine	August 24–September 2
Willow	September 3–September 12
Lime	September 13–September 22
Olive	September 23
Hazel	September 24–October 3
Mountain Ash	October 4–October 13
Maple	October 14–October 22
Walnut	October 23–November 2
Yew	November 3–November 11
Chestnut	November 12–November 21
Mountain Ash	November 22–December 1
Hornbeam	December 2–December 11
Fig	December 12–December 22
Apple	December 23–January 1

Norse Runic Astrology

The runes are letters of an ancient alphabet; individual letters were traditionally cut onto slices of wood or written on smooth pebbles. The word *rune* means "mystery," "secret," or "whisper," and each rune has, in addition to its everyday meaning, esoteric meanings and properties attached to it. The runes originate in northern Europe and Scandinavia. They were devised by people from the Teutonic tribes, and their use spread into the Scandinavian Viking tribes and early Germanic ones, such as the Saxons.

Tradition has it that the god Odin hung himself upside down from the sacred tree, Yggdrasil. He stayed like this for nine days, during which time he reached enlightenment. At this point, he discovered the runes lying among the roots of the tree, and he was led to understand their divinatory meanings and their alphabet.

It is interesting to note that this is the only form of astrology that arises out of the need to devise an alphabet—most of the other astrological systems arose from the need to develop a usable calendar. Differences in the way the names of the runes are pronounced and spelled reflect whether the origin of the word is Teutonic, Saxon, or Norse/Viking.

The meanings behind the runes are derived partly from the agriculture, weather, geography, and plant life of northern Europe and Scandinavia, and partly from the myths and legends surrounding pagan gods such as Thor, Freya, and Odin.

Each rune sign runs for a period of two weeks.

There are twenty-four runes in the alphabet, so this fits quite well into an annual system; the extra four weeks are taken up by the sign of Hagalaz, assigned to the Halloween period, and Jera, the sign associated with beginnings and endings, which encompasses Christmas and the period just before the New Year.

Look up your birth month in the "A–Z of Astrology" section to read the astrological significance of the Norse rune that applies to your birth date.

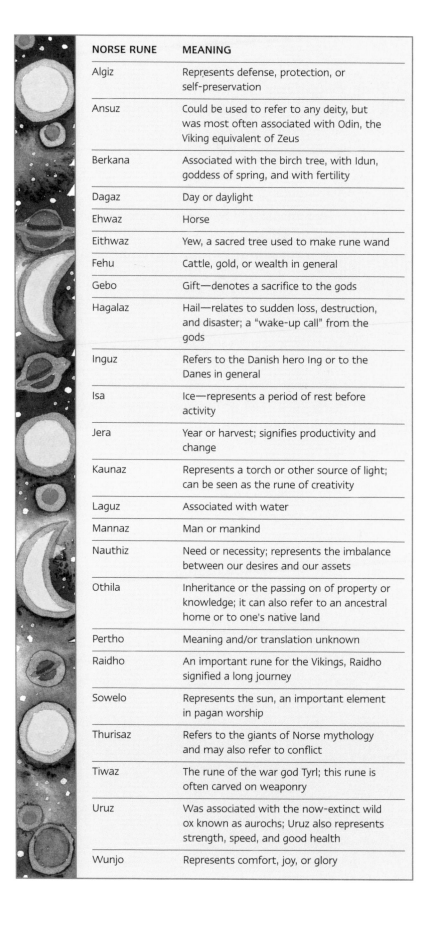

NORSE RUNE	MEANING
Algiz	Represents defense, protection, or self-preservation
Ansuz	Could be used to refer to any deity, but was most often associated with Odin, the Viking equivalent of Zeus
Berkana	Associated with the birch tree, with Idun, goddess of spring, and with fertility
Dagaz	Day or daylight
Ehwaz	Horse
Eithwaz	Yew, a sacred tree used to make rune wand
Fehu	Cattle, gold, or wealth in general
Gebo	Gift—denotes a sacrifice to the gods
Hagalaz	Hail—relates to sudden loss, destruction, and disaster; a "wake-up call" from the gods
Inguz	Refers to the Danish hero Ing or to the Danes in general
Isa	Ice—represents a period of rest before activity
Jera	Year or harvest; signifies productivity and change
Kaunaz	Represents a torch or other source of light; can be seen as the rune of creativity
Laguz	Associated with water
Mannaz	Man or mankind
Nauthiz	Need or necessity; represents the imbalance between our desires and our assets
Othila	Inheritance or the passing on of property or knowledge; it can also refer to an ancestral home or to one's native land
Pertho	Meaning and/or translation unknown
Raidho	An important rune for the Vikings, Raidho signified a long journey
Sowelo	Represents the sun, an important element in pagan worship
Thurisaz	Refers to the giants of Norse mythology and may also refer to conflict
Tiwaz	The rune of the war god Tyrl; this rune is often carved on weaponry
Uruz	Was associated with the now-extinct wild ox known as aurochs; Uruz also represents strength, speed, and good health
Wunjo	Represents comfort, joy, or glory

West African Astrology

North Africa is home to Egyptian and Arab peoples, as well as to a number of other races, particularly along the periphery of the continent, where traders, colonists, slavers, and imported workers all settled. In these areas, writing and record keeping do exist—usually in Arabic. Most Africans who live in the countryside in the center and south of the continent still study the sky for weather patterns, inspiration, and divinatory purposes, and have no written language.

West Africa has a tradition of geomancy similar to that used in ancient Egyptian sand reading. The shaman, or wise man, chooses a patch of ground at the approach to the village and outlines this with sticks in a form that resembles a miniature airstrip. Pieces of string are threaded across the strip overnight. The following morning the wise man inspects the area and studies the tracks made by animals walking over it during the night.

The original ancient Egyptian method eventually became formalized and incorporated into zodiac astrology. Napoleon Bonaparte, a great collector of occult knowledge, discovered a form of this, which became known as the Oracle of Napoleon. The designs used in the Egyptian method and those of the West African astrology system are very similar.

Look up your birth month in the "A–Z of Astrology" section to find the astrological significance of the West African symbol that applies on your birth date.

WEST AFRICAN SYMBOL	PERIOD OF INFLUENCE
The Baobab Tree	January 4–February 3
The Wealth of Amber and Silver	February 4–March 4
The Family	March 5–April 3
Small Services to the Neighborhood	April 4–May 4
The Market	May 5–June 3
The Ancestor	June 4–July 4
The Judge	July 5–August 4
The Kola Nut	August 5–September 3
The Traveler	September 4–October 3
The Distance	October 4–November 3
The Child of the World	November 4–December 3
The Harvest and the Granary	December 4–January 3

Ancient Egyptian and Israeli Astrology

ANCIENT EGYPTIAN ASTROLOGY

Many different forms of astrology were developed in Ancient Egypt, all predating the Western zodiac and rising sign system. One of the earliest was linked to the movement of the Moon—this lives on in an adapted form in Arabic astrology and Vedic astrology as the Mansions of the Moon. One slight difference between the two systems is that the Vedic uses twenty-seven lunar signs while the Arabic uses twenty-eight. Later forms of Egyptian astrology were far more like the Western zodiac system.

THE THEBAIC CALENDAR

Another system is the Thebaic Calendar. This calendar was used in the city of Thebes when the city was at the height of its power. The Thebaic system divides the ecliptic into ninety divisions, with four degrees each. Each of these had a little illustration, or hieroglyph, and each had its own meaning.

HEBREW ASTROLOGY

Hebrew astrology assigns letters of the Hebrew alphabet to each sign of the zodiac, as well as to each planet. The number of letters in the alphabet varies a little depending upon which tradition is used, but nineteen letters will cover the basics, corresponding to twelve signs plus the seven planets visible to the naked eye. These letters were mainly used in Hebrew numerology, which, like Chinese astrology, might have had its origins in the stars, planets, and constellations, but evolved over the years to become far more attached to numbers and their meanings.

APRIL

APRIL ~ ARIES
FROM THE 1ST TO THE 20TH

The extroverted fire sign of Aries gives you great courage and optimism, and you get things done. The honest, humorous, and outspoken nature of Aries is echoed by the Dragon of Chinese astrology, which, being active and earth, enables you to build for the future and lead others. The Vedic sign of Meena brings a softening touch, an intuitive and spiritual element, and a strong belief system.

The first mansion in April is Krittika, which brings success, eminence, and fame—it can also be associated with political events that sometimes overtake your life. This changes to Rohini, which brings honor, intelligence, eloquence, and public acclaim, after which Mrigashira takes over; this also brings honor, as a result of civil or military work.

The Native American Red Hawk of the Thunderbird clan makes you a friendly and generous person, and a strong and capable leader. This changes on the last day to the Beaver of the Turtle clan, which is slower to act and keen to improve the environment. The

West African sign of the Family also encourages you to look after your community and area, but this soon changes to the sign of Small Services to the Neighborhood; people in this sign have to learn how to act with judgment on behalf of others.

The Celtic sign of the Mountain Ash makes you a little secretive at times, tough in business, but kind to friends and family. The change to the Maple means increased powers of leadership and ambition, but with a soft spot for your loved ones. The Norse runic sign of Ehwaz adds nobility, but with a hint of a wild streak beneath the surface. This changes to Mannaz, which brings a humanitarian streak and an interest in scientific or spiritual matters.

APRIL ~ TAURUS
FROM THE 21ST ONWARD

The earth sign of Taurus makes you reliable, sensible, practical, and honest. You have an artistic streak, and you work well with your hands. The active earth element of your Chinese sign enhances this practicality, but also brings executive ability and a refusal to allow the grass to grow under your feet. The Chinese Dragon ensures that you are strong and stubborn, but your delightful sense of humor and kindness ensure your popularity.

The Vedic sign of Mesha adds a sprinkling of enterprise and ambition, plus the ability to lead others and work for the betterment of others, although you would never neglect your own needs while doing so. The mansion of Mrigashira ensures that you earn honors through working for the public or in the civil or military arena.

The Native American Beaver is known for hard work and obstinacy in the face of failure. You take your responsibilities to your family seriously, and you lavish affection and attention on those you love, although you don't hesitate to argue with them when you have a point to make. The West African sign of Small Services to the Neighborhood ensures that you will have to make decisions on behalf of others. This also prevents you from jumping into anything without thinking about it first.

Your Celtic tree sign is Walnut, which makes you realistic, sensible, hardworking, and courageous. You are undoubtedly a family person, and the results of your efforts in the outside world can be seen in your nice home and well-cared-for family. However, you can be a little materialistic. Your Norse runic sign is Laguz, which brings a completely different energy and makes you empathic, understanding, open-minded, and caring. You will remain young-looking throughout your life.

AQUARIUS

JANUARY 20 TO FEBRUARY 18
SYMBOL: THE WATER CARRIER
RULING PLANET: URANUS
GROUPS: POSITIVE, AIR, FIXED

Being highly independent, you like doing things your own way, but you can always be swayed by logical argument. You are both a traditionalist and a person who has the ability to understand the trends of the future. You are able to walk comfortably between the past and the future.

You are reasonable, humorous, friendly, and trusting, until someone hurts you. Your sense of humor tends toward the quirky and the eccentric, and you enjoy the unusual and the strange.

You are comfortable both as a loner and as a part of a group. You are the type of friend people turn to when they need perceptive advice and are not afraid of the truth. You tend not to be very tactful, and you see no reason to pull punches with either friends or work colleagues, but you will generally not do this maliciously.

One of the challenges that Aquarians must master is to not be oversensitive in a group situation—you may feel insecure and lash out against your friends, generating hostility and distrust instead of the approval you crave.

Being highly intelligent and fond of gadgets, your inventive mind will take you into the world of new technology or offbeat ideas, echoing your fondness for the bizarre and the new.

Being an air sign, your career choices often include flying (perhaps being a pilot) or doing something that is associated with communication, such as being a radio broadcaster. Music and writing also interest you. Famous Aquarians in the music and literary fields include Wolfgang Amadeus Mozart, James Joyce, and Gertrude Stein.

Your highly developed skills of intuition can lead you into New Age areas such as astrology or clairvoyance; your ability to focus and to pursue intellectual interests can lead you into the study of a science such as aeronautics.

At work, you may find that although you can easily work with the established system, you also have the ability to improve the system or to invent new ways of doing or thinking about your work. Famous Aquarian scientists include Charles Darwin.

You feel that life is too interesting to spend your time worrying about money or practicalities, although you can solve these problems when you have to. You are generally nonmaterialistic, but you usually like what you have to be of good quality. Another challenge is to bring your thoughts and ideas to reality—you tend to think abstractly, so you may need to improve your ability to make your ideas workable.

At home, you are a loving but possibly careless homemaker, preferring to make intriguing toys for your children than to plump up cushions. You enjoy performing a variety of roles in the home, depending on your mood. Aquarians tend to be a bit inconsistent in their roles as parents and lovers.

Intimacy in relationships is always a challenge for Aquarians. You operate best in a relationship where your partner allows you to be free and independent. Consistent one-to-one relationships need work, but you have the charm and compassion of a great humanitarian within you, and this will help you conquer your relationship problems and fears.

You need a partner who understands your quirky ways and is independent. You tend not to be a terribly passionate person, and you seek partners who can inspire your mind rather than your body.

ASTROLOGICAL COMPATIBILITY

WHAT SUN SIGN ARE YOU? Aquarius

WHO ARE YOUR FRIENDS? Aries, Sagittarius

WHO ARE YOUR LOVERS? Gemini, Scorpio

ARIES

MARCH 21 TO APRIL 20
SYMBOL: THE RAM
RULING PLANET: MARS
GROUPS: POSITIVE, FIRE, CARDINAL

Some Arians come across as loud, while others are quiet and reserved; either way, you don't allow the grass to grow under your feet. You are ambitious for all the best things in life, and you feel frustrated if they sometimes do not manifest all at once for you. You are impulsive, which can help you get what others are too afraid to even ask for!

You tend not to feel restraint or fear when you set upon a new goal or purpose in life. However, you can be prone to doubt if you meet too many obstacles. Sometimes, Arians are accused of being unable to finish what they set out to achieve. This can arise because you did not plan well enough in advance or understand the full ramifications of your impulsive adoption of a particular course of action.

However, you are not afraid of hard work. You are competitive both at work and in your hobbies, and you can gain a high position in life through a combination of consistent effort and adroit political skills. One famous Arian was Thomas Jefferson. You are definitely the leader of the pack. You don't feel particularly comfortable in a group unless you have gathered your friends or colleagues together for a particular purpose or function.

If you are doing something that you believe in, you will have no end of courage to meet the challenges that face you. You tend to be forthright and assertive, even in quiet ways. As you are a straightforward person, subtleties are boring to you; you would rather take action to deal with a problem than think and talk

---

ASTROLOGICAL COMPATIBILITY

WHAT SUN SIGN ARE YOU? Aries

WHO ARE YOUR FRIENDS? Gemini, Aquarius

WHO ARE YOUR LOVERS? Leo, Sagittarius

through what needs to be done. This can lead to either decisive victories or heroic failures through lack of forethought!

You are keen on art and music, but you are unlikely to work in these fields. You seek to make a mark in the world in a profession or calling where you will be heard and respected. Politics, writing, and law are areas that will attract you, particularly if you are interested in protecting the rights of others. You tend to generate conflict and can revel in it, possibly a little too much if you are feeling bored in other areas of your life.

You may sometimes come across as domineering—knowing what you want and having the self-confidence to get it. An Arian may sometimes be capable of being insensitive with regard to the feelings of others. An Arian challenge is to try to avoid controlling others.

Passion is your ruler, both in terms of love and sex and in terms of what you believe to be important. Although you tend to find it difficult to settle on a particular life partner, once you have made a commitment you generally stick to it. You try hard in marriage and love your children deeply. Consistent passion is a challenge for Arians, as they become bored quite quickly.

Like the element that is associated with this star sign, Arians constantly need stimulation—in terms of new people and new ideas—to keep them interested. Arians particularly dislike boredom and will go a long way to avoid it.

AUGUST

AUGUST ~ LEO
FROM THE 1ST TO THE 23RD

The passionate and fiery sign of Leo is in evidence now, so generosity, humor, and kindness rule, along with great love for your children and pets. You are easily irritated by fools or by those who seek to get in your way. The Chinese sign of the Monkey gives you an inventive mind and great commercial ability, while the active metal element makes you difficult to persuade or influence.

The Vedic sign of Karkarta adds a softening layer of intuition and sensitivity, and it also makes it imperative that you have a home you can come back to. The Vedic mansion of Uttara Phalguni suggests a quick mind, a generous nature, and the chance to achieve high honor. This changes to the mansion of Hasta, which indicates charm and a successful life, although you can suddenly fall out of favor.

The Native American Salmon of the Thunderbird clan gives you a slightly regal air—but it hides a sensitive nature. At the end of this period, this changes to the Brown Bear of the Turtle clan, which indicates a cool exterior, but a soft heart. The West African sign of the Judge begins this period, denoting a strong will and the ability to learn from experience. This soon changes to the clairvoyant and sensitive sign of the Kola Nut.

The Celtic tree signs open with the Cypress, which indicates a need to be appreciated for who you are, but this soon changes to the Poplar, which indicates that you vacillate between fulfilling your own needs and those of others. The final Celtic tree, Cedar, belongs to a bubbly, enterprising personality. The Norse runic signs are the strong Thurisaz, which bestows leadership and ability, and then Ansuz, whose influence gives you a deep yearning for eternal values.

AUGUST ~ VIRGO
FROM THE 24TH ONWARD

The practical and intellectual earth sign of Virgo denotes literary and communication skills, a talent for research, and an eye for detail, but with the perfectionist's tendency to worry over insignificant details. The Chinese sign of the active metal Monkey adds independence, strength, common sense, commercial ability, and a talent for getting jobs done. There are times when you may work far too hard for your own good.

The Vedic sign of Karkarta suggests a cautious nature, an eye for business, and a need for a strong home and family life. This changes to Simha, which indicates creativity in art and business, and the ability to make a happy home. Simha can also add a touch of arrogance or pomposity to your nature. The Vedic mansion of Chitra brings success, which can lead to wealth, plus a deep love of science and the arts.

The Native American Brown Bear of the Turtle clan gives you a cheerful nature and an excellent sense of humor, and it makes you keen to discover as much as possible about everything. The only real drawback is a tendency to take on lame ducks or try to rescue those who are beyond help. The West African sign of the Kola Nut indicates a desire to make changes just for the sake of changing, but this sign also gives you intuition, which helps with decision making.

The Celtic tree is the Pine, which makes you reserved, introverted, modest, and quiet, but still a little more egotistical than others realize. You are also more sensitive than you let on. The Norse runic sign of Ansuz adds eloquence and a spiritual outlook; Raidho reveals a character with a noble spirit, a seeker after truth.

B

BEAVER

Native Americans view Beavers as nature's prime example of industriousness. Beaver dams are engineering feats, cleverly created to provide the animal with many entries and exits so that it is secure from its enemies.

Beavers spend much of their time working on their dams, and little time at play. Beaver people are extremely practical, hardworking individuals who demonstrate an almost unlimited abundance of patience, whether at work on individual tasks or in the company of others.

They expect high standards of performance from themselves and others. Yet they are not stressed by deadlines, as they apply themselves methodically and commit others to a clear action plan that will get everyone there in the end. Beavers are extremely task-focused, operating at the material level. Hence, they don't come

SEASON	The heart of springtime—a time of rapid growth
SEASON TOTEM	Eagle
SEASON ELEMENT	Fire
BIRTH TIME	April 20–May 20 Northern Hemisphere October 23–November 21 Southern Hemisphere
BIRTH TIME ELEMENT	Earth
ELEMENTAL CLAN	Turtle
ENERGY FLOW	Receptive
AFFINITIES	Color: blue Plant: lily Mineral: turquoise
GIFTS	Tenacity, practicality, steadfastness, industriousness, patience, reliability, dexterity
CHALLENGES	Overindulgence, stubbornness, overly opinionated, inflexible
LIFE PATH	To embrace emotions readily and express them constantly, thus avoiding a totally logical approach to life.

across as big talkers, travelers, or socializers. Beavers' families and homes are extremely important to them. They will readily commit whatever is required—money, time, or anything else—in order to make their hearth secure.

Their energy type is reflective, which means they like to think before they act. They have the capacity to embrace the emotional, nurturing side of life; beavers do feel deeply about their lives and the people in them. However, they can have a difficult time expressing and demonstrating their feelings.

IDEAL PAIRINGS	
Beaver +	Relationship potential
Brown Bear	Both are industrious and reliable. Much can be accomplished and accumulated when Beaver and Brown Bear get together.
Snow Goose	Both are hardworking and practical-minded; hence, each will respect the other's loyalty and dedication throughout life.
Wolf	Wolf will gain materialistically from a union with the industrious Beaver. Beaver will admire Wolf's philosophical and spiritual approach to life.
Woodpecker	Woodpecker's loving nature and devotion will be enough to soften the usually inflexible nature of Beaver, who will reward Woodpecker with material security.
Snake	**Complement.** A natural attraction and kinship exists between these two animal totems. Each will make the other a loyal and supportive companion.

CHALLENGING PAIRINGS	
Beaver +	Relationship potential
Otter	They live on opposite sides of the stream. Beaver is industrious and prefers to work. Otter is imaginative and prefers to play.
Hawk	Steadfast Beaver will come into the relationship with set opinions. Hawk will want to take a more liberal approach. They will soon part.
Deer	Deer will prove too sensitive and coy for the tenacious and opinionated Beaver. Beaver and Deer are rarely attracted to each other—their natures are worlds apart.
Salmon	Salmon will want excitement and sensual stimulation from Beaver, and Beaver will want practicality and hard work. Both will end up empty-handed.
Raven	Influential Raven achieves success through others, while Beaver achieves success through sheer hard work. There will be no appreciation for each other's tactics.
Owl	Each will want to dominate the other in this relationship. Beaver will remain inflexible despite Owl's attempts to exert influence, and Owl will be too proud to give Beaver any ground.
Beaver	Beaver pairing with another will bring about a mirroring effect, whereby the best and the worst in each other will be magnified.

BROWN BEAR

The sheer size and strength of brown bears gives
them a great deal of magnetism and presence.
Native Americans have due respect for the brown
bear, admiring its hunting skills and the strong
protection it gives its young.

When Brown Bears are at their best they are
hardworking, discerning, and tenacious. They
often demonstrate good judgment in their decision
making, and are fair and considerate when dealing
with others. Where there is a problem, when someone
is in distress, or even when something is broken,
Brown Bears feel it their responsibility to fix it all. In
fact, they may have the talent to fix just about anything.

Like their animal totem, Brown Bears have a strong physical
presence. They attract the attention of others by their courage in
standing up for what they believe is fair and just, and they make
loyal and protective friends, family members, and work colleagues.
Their particular gifts lie in their considered approach to life and
their perseverance. They are realistic, practical, analytical, and
deliberate people who demonstrate good sense and self-reliance.
Brown Bears can rise to meet any challenge life throws at them.

SEASON	Late summer—harvesting time, a time to reap what has been sown
SEASON TOTEM	Coyote
SEASON ELEMENT	Water
BIRTH TIME	August 23–September 22 Northern Hemisphere February 19–March 20 Southern Hemisphere
BIRTH TIME ELEMENT	Earth
ELEMENTAL CLAN	Turtle
ENERGY FLOW	Receptive
AFFINITIES	Color: purple Plant: violet Mineral: amethyst
GIFTS	Perseverance, judgment, fairness and justice, powers of discrimination, responsibility, common sense, courage, wisdom
CHALLENGES	Cynicism, critical nature, aloofness, conventionalism
LIFE PATH	To provide space in your life to nurture the spiritual core and in the process achieve the ultimate—balance between the physical, emotional, and spiritual planes.

Seeing a Brown Bear triumph through a difficult time is a vision of pure perseverance in action. While they are at their best in the physical world, Brown Bears also have a natural tie to the world of the heart and the emotions. So, as well as being physically magnificent, Brown Bears are at the same time gentle, warm, caring, cheerful, and good-natured.

IDEAL PAIRINGS

Brown Bear +	Relationship potential
Snow Goose	Both are dedicated and methodical individuals who will provide each other with the support and encouragement they desire for their endeavors.
Beaver	Both are industrious and reliable. Much can be accomplished and accumulated when Beaver and Brown Bear get together.
Woodpecker	There will be an immediate attraction—Brown Bear will be unable to resist Woodpecker's generous and loyal nature, and Woodpecker will enjoy Brown Bear's courage and perseverance.
Snake	Both are patient and wise individuals who will be able to see the numerous benefits in the relationship before physical attraction has even taken hold.
Wolf	**Complement.** A natural attraction and kinship exists between these two animal totems. Each will make the other a loyal and supportive companion.

CHALLENGING PAIRINGS

Brown Bear +	Relationship potential
Otter	Otters are optimistic daredevils, while Brown Bears are cynical and far too serious. Neither will meet the other's expectations.
Hawk	Impulsive Hawk will find the methodical Brown Bear stodgy and stifling. Brown Bear will soon be openly criticizing Hawk's impulsive behavior.
Deer	Where Brown Bear will persevere, Deer will prefer to give in. When Deer is in need of affection, Brown Bear will be aloof. These two will have little in common.
Salmon	Cheerful Salmon will not be impressed with Brown Bear's cynicism, and Brown Bear will be too critical of Salmon's wayward charm and sensuality.
Raven	Brown Bear will grow critical of Raven's idealistic goals and charitable inclinations. Raven will find Brown Bear lacking in enthusiasm.
Owl	These two opinionated and strong-willed individuals will clash on meeting. They will end up as adversaries in most situations.
Brown Bear	Brown Bear pairing with another will bring about a mirroring effect, whereby the best and the worst in each other will be magnified.

■ FOR **BUFFALO** (CHINESE ASTROLOGY), SEE **OX** ON PAGES 128–31.

CANCER

JUNE 22 TO JULY 22
SYMBOL: THE CRAB
RULING PLANET: THE MOON
GROUPS: NEGATIVE, WATER, CARDINAL

Your basic nature is cautious and protective: you don't enjoy taking crazy chances, and you hate the thought of your family being in any kind of trouble. You are a great nurturer, always caring for your friends and extended family, looking out for their welfare, and remembering their likes and dislikes. Cancerians usually have fabulous memories, but this trait may sometimes lead them to remember slights and disagreements that should have been forgotten and forgiven long ago.

On the positive side, the Cancerian combination of love of the past and an ability to retain vast amounts of information can lead to particular career paths, such as being a historian or a writer. You have a responsible and sensible attitude to your working life, often choosing a job that puts you in touch with the public and which supplies some of their needs. Jobs in the hospitality industry usually suit you admirably.

You are slow to fall in love and steadfast once you have done so, because you take all relationships seriously. You are very caring in your relationships—and are a generous lover—and particularly enjoy being with those who provide you with emotional stability.

ASTROLOGICAL COMPATIBILITY

WHAT SUN SIGN ARE YOU? Cancer

WHO ARE YOUR FRIENDS? Taurus, Virgo

WHO ARE YOUR LOVERS? Scorpio, Pisces

You have a magnetic personality and can attract quite a lot of attention. Cancerians enjoy being the center of attention, but they expect their generosity to be returned.

If you feel that you are being ignored or that someone has hurt you, you can become somewhat moody and hard to fathom. If you are feeling insecure, you may tend to withdraw and make it difficult for the person who hurt you to make amends and to set things straight.

Your challenge is to not withdraw or become defensive when challenged or confronted, but to stand your ground and resolve the issue. Use your great perceptive abilities to help you understand the problems facing you and find ways of overcoming them.

You enjoy travel and novelty, but you also love coming home again. You take great pride in your home, and your house is always well looked after and filled with objects that give you a sense of the past. You usually love antiques, especially things that were actually made by your ancestors. You will always be complimented on your attractively comfortable home, and your guests will often stay longer than you expect them to. You may even become a talented interior decorator or designer.

You also like the good things in life and can acquire a reputation as a gourmand. Your love of entertaining at home may well lead you to be a gourmet chef yourself! Cancerians are generally materialistic and need to feel financially secure. They will tend not to indulge in risky investments but will seek to build up their finances slowly and steadily. In this way you will be able to prosper as a businessperson. Famous Cancerian businessmen include John D. Rockefeller.

CAPRICORN

DECEMBER 22 TO JANUARY 19
SYMBOL: THE GOAT
RULING PLANET: SATURN
GROUPS: NEGATIVE, EARTH, CARDINAL

Some of you are outgoing and happy to be in the limelight, and others are shy and retiring, but all of you are ambitious to have a good life. Your ambitions may be just for yourself, but they are often also for your family, your employers, or your country. You are very focused in following your goals, but finding the right goal to pursue can sometimes be difficult.

You may find that you have too much choice or that the goal that you have set is not exactly the right one. If you have too many options, you may find that you procrastinate and do nothing. However, if you are following the wrong path, you may find it extremely difficult to stop and change directions.

Usually, the more difficult the goal, the more attractive it looks to you. You would be better off to resist doing things the hard way purely for the sake of it—use your sensitivity and perceptiveness to identify your skills and abilities, and use these as an indication of your true path in life. Famous Capricornians include Sir Isaac Newton, Benjamin Franklin, Howard Hughes, and J. Edgar Hoover.

Being a hard and reliable worker, you are usually respected and appreciated for what you do, but you can be fussy or demanding. You are an excellent manager and have a talent for motivating your staff. You have a great sense of practicality and are capable of building great wealth, although you are not greatly motivated by materialism.

In love, you want a total relationship and to be secure in the knowledge that you come first. You do not rush into relationships;

ASTROLOGICAL COMPATIBILITY

WHAT SUN SIGN ARE YOU? Capricorn
WHO ARE YOUR FRIENDS? Scorpio, Pisces
WHO ARE YOUR LOVERS? Taurus, Virgo

you prefer to take your time and weigh up the pros and cons of being with a particular person. When you are happy in a relationship, you are caring, protective, and very loving. However, if you feel insecure or are made to feel that you are duty-bound to stay in a difficult relationship, you turn morose and taciturn. You are generally self-sufficient, and you tend to withdraw within yourself to guard your sensitive nature.

Sometimes Capricornians can withdraw so far that they become detached from reality and obsessed with the past. They can also find it hard to communicate with those around them. It is not surprising that Elvis Presley is another famous Capricornian.

You adore your children and are a faithful and dependable partner. You enjoy travel, but you love coming home again. You yearn for a peaceful home life and will become withdrawn and detached if you feel powerless to achieve this. The challenge for Capricornians is to express what they need; they must learn communication skills because it is important not to suffer in silence.

■ FOR **CAT** (CHINESE ASTROLOGY), SEE **RABBIT** ON PAGES 138–41.

■ FOR **CHICKEN** (CHINESE ASTROLOGY), SEE **ROOSTER** ON PAGES 148–51.

D

DECEMBER

DECEMBER ~ SAGITTARIUS
FROM THE 1ST TO THE 21ST

The month opens with the cheerful, friendly, fiery sign of Sagittarius, which indicates a need for freedom in both your personal relationships and in your working life. The Chinese sign

for December is the active water Rat, which allows you to succeed against appalling odds. The active water element adds commercial and financial sense.

The Vedic sign of Vrishchika helps you keep secrets and your innermost feelings under wraps and signifies intelligence, intuition, and caution. The first mansion is Uttarashada, which endows you with leadership qualities in business or public life; it also suggests a strong sense of music and rhythm. This changes to Shravana, which denotes a courageous and ambitious nature that puts you in positions of leadership. The last mansion is Dhanishta, which indicates intuition and an interest in astrology.

Your Native American sign is the Elk of the Thunderbird clan. This gives you a regal air and a tendency to keep your feelings hidden inside. The West African Child of the World sign ensures that you take your duties toward others seriously and that you can attract the help of others when it is needed. The later sign, the Harvest and the Granary, means you are a little complacent when life is easy.

The Celtic tree sign of the Mountain Ash leads you into the wrong kinds of love relationships until you learn better. This changes to the Hornbeam, which indicates charm and a cheerful, friendly personality. The Fig signifies sex appeal, independence, and a deep understanding of human nature. The Norse runic sign of Isa means that you are emotionally cool and contained and able to work toward a specific objective. This changes to Jera, which brings luck and a happy home.

DECEMBER ~ CAPRICORN
FROM THE 22ND ONWARD

The earth sign of Capricorn means that your ambitions are as much for your family as for yourself. You know that life can be difficult, so you work hard and take a sensible attitude to money. The Chinese sign of the Rat adds a quiet air that belies your intelligence and determination. The active water element ensures that you have common sense, a talent for communication, and good business sense.

The Vedic sign for late December starts with Vrishchika, which suggests that your passions run deep and that you are more sensual than you appear. This changes to the outgoing Dhanus, which brings a touch of adventure and humor to your personality. Your mansion is Dhanishta, which lends you intuition and an interest in astrology— it can also make you an excellent writer or take you into a career in public affairs.

Your Native American sign is the Snow Goose of the Turtle clan. This sign means that your mind is able to roam freely while your feet stay firmly on the ground. Your sensitive feelings can make you see an insult where none is intended. The West African sign of the Harvest and the Granary ensures that you save for a rainy day and are prepared for lean times.

The Celtic tree sign of the Apple brings an appreciation of art and a strong need to protect your home and family from harm. This changes to the Beech, which brings elegance and ambition, but also a slightly standoffish appearance to those who don't know you well. The Norse runic sign of Jera brings luck and a need for a happy home; this changes later to Eihwaz, which can make you fussy and a little possessive, but also farsighted, and protective of weaker people.

DEER

Deer are beautiful to behold, and Native Americans have esteemed them for this quality, as well as for their natural grace, gentleness, and agility. Coming upon a deer or fawn was a sign for the Native American that you should stop and appreciate the beauty and love you have in your life.

Deer people are beautiful both physically and spiritually, as they radiate love and concern for others in all their thoughts, words, and actions. Naturally, they are attracted to all things beautiful themselves and will often possess works of art and numerous items of colorful clothing. Nature and the great outdoors also attract the attention of gentle Deer people.

Deer are also skillful with language and have quick minds and good intuition. They possess the gift of gab and appear quite jovial and witty when in the company of others. Many Deer are often termed "socialites."

Deer just love company, and they are much more energized when they are around others than when they are on their own.

SEASON	Late spring—a time of expansion and flowering, of color and beauty
SEASON TOTEM	Eagle
SEASON ELEMENT	Fire
BIRTH TIME	May 21–June 20 Northern Hemisphere November 22–December 21 Southern Hemisphere
BIRTH TIME ELEMENT	Air
ELEMENTAL CLAN	Butterfly
ENERGY FLOW	Active
AFFINITIES	Color: green Plant: yarrow Mineral: moss agate (a type of quartz)
GIFTS	Grace, gentleness, sensitivity, beauty, versatility, alertness, intuitiveness, wittiness, joviality
CHALLENGES	Nervousness, restlessness, disorganization, talkativeness
LIFE PATH	To take life more seriously when necessary and to focus on preparation and organization in daily life.

Given their active type of energy, Deer like to be kept busy and entertained.

Deer are colorful and entertaining to others, and very accepting of other people's viewpoints and situations. Deer have no interest in changing other people—their focus is on being socially desirable themselves.

IDEAL PAIRINGS

Deer +	Relationship potential
Otter	This pair has the potential for a fun-filled and harmonious life together. There is little capacity for friction in either.
Raven	This pair will exude grace and charm. They are both active, and will be quite communicative with one another.
Deer	Hawk will provide Deer with boldness and foresight, while Deer will encourage Hawk's gentler side.
Salmon	Both are versatile, and this will be mutually attractive. Deer will be happy to be directed by the determined Salmon, who will bestow much affection on Deer.
Owl	**Complement.** A natural attraction and kinship exists between these two animal totems. Each will make the other a loyal and supportive companion.

CHALLENGING PAIRINGS

Deer +	Relationship potential
Wolf	Both can be extremely nervous types. They may experience high anxiety while in a relationship together.
Snow Goose	Snow Goose will find Deer superficial, and Deer will soon be dismissed. Deer will be too easily hurt by Snow Goose's arrogance.
Beaver	Deer will prove too sensitive and coy for the tenacious and opinionated Beaver. Beaver and Deer are rarely attracted to each other—their natures are worlds apart.
Woodpecker	Both are prone to nervousness and insecurity. Theirs would be a vulnerable relationship, lacking in any real support and practicality.
Brown Bear	Where Brown Bear will persevere, Deer will prefer to give in. When Deer is in need of affection, Brown Bear will be aloof. These two will have little in common.
Snake	Snake can take the hard knocks in life, while Deer has a tendency to falter. Snake will think Deer weak, and Deer will think Snake too rigid and critical.
Deer	Deer pairing with another Deer will bring about a mirroring effect, whereby the best and the worst in each other will be magnified.

DOG

THE JUST, LOYAL DOG
1922, 1934, 1946, 1958, 1970, 1982, 1994, 2006, 2018
ENERGY: YANG
ELEMENT: EARTH
TIME: 7:00 P.M.–9:00 P.M.
MONTH: OCTOBER
DIRECTION: WEST/NORTHWEST
SEASON: LATE FALL

Dogs are loyal, principled, and just. They are the humanitarians and protectors of the Chinese zodiac. They live according to a strong code of ethics and are usually greatly admired and appreciated by others. Dogs take life seriously. They are perpetually pursuing their compulsion to address the injustices of the world, and they will follow this path even if it means they have to sacrifice their own needs and desires.

Patient and watchful, Dogs operate by instinct and will choose the right time to act rather than rushing into something unknown. As long as Dogs have a cause to stand for, they will not be overwhelmed by the pessimism to which they are prone.

The Dog ascendant for those born between 7:00 P.M. and 9:00 P.M. This ascendant sign will impart an ethical, principled nature. Those with the Dog as the ascendant sign are loyal and just in their dealings with others.

Dogs at their best Concerned, compassionate, driven, loyal, principled, protective, responsible, idealistic, trustworthy

Dogs at their worst Anxious, pessimistic, judgmental, distrustful, discouraging, cynical, introverted

Character traits of Dogs Loyal, dutiful, unselfish, honest, idealistic, courageous, trustworthy, tolerant, faithful, responsible, anxious, capable, honorable, kind, generous, compassionate, heroic

Dog's eleventh position at Buddha's side stands for loyalty and justice. People born in Dog years are idealistic and highly principled. They have strong beliefs and live by their morals. To a Dog, everything in life is either black or white, right or wrong, good or bad—there is no middle ground. Dogs hate injustice, insincerity, and disloyalty.

Life challenge for Dogs To love and care for themselves, and to learn to ask for what they want.

The Dog lover Dogs make thoughtful and loyal lovers who take their time falling in love. Dog lovers are more affectionate than passionate and can easily become hurt and depressed by the words and actions of their lovers. Once Dogs commit, they become deeply attached to their partners and can be a little possessive. Dogs' partners will need to reward their faithful Dog lovers with lots of praise and reassurance, to relieve them of their general anxiety about the relationship and their jealousy and suspiciousness.

The Dog family member Children can identify with Dogs' basic nature—friendly, straightforward, playful—and hence adore their Dog parent. Likewise, Dog parents adore their children. Good communication and strong relationships exist in Dog households, as Dogs are patient and good listeners. Dogs also make good providers for their families and are not above sacrificing their own dreams and desires to provide for their partners and children. In China it is the Dogs who are the ultimate family protectors, and any family lucky enough to contain a Dog parent will be blessed with much security and comfort.

The Dog friend Dogs appear a little reserved, even aloof, in large gatherings, and do not make friends instantly. They prefer to play keen observer for a while, deciding who they like before approaching them for friendly conversation and more thoroughly assessing their natures. Once Dogs make friends, they are loyal and trusting to those friends for life. While generous with their own time and possessions, they will not ask for much in return, and are quite understanding about and forgiving of any faults in their friends.

The Dog at work More than anything, Dogs need to be proud of their professions, so they seek meaningful work. They are usually involved in humanitarian or social justice causes. They like responsibility and clear direction, preferably in a team environment. Dogs are not materialistic and are motivated more by their personal sense of achievement than they are by money. Dogs are not good left on their own. Dogs are respected and much confided in by their employers and colleagues because of their tireless hard work, competent decision making, and devotion to the organization. These traits alone will see many Dogs quickly and effortlessly reach high positions.

Ideal occupations for Dogs Charity worker, missionary, attorney, judge, doctor, police officer, religious leader

The five Dog types

WOOD DOGS • 1934, 1994 • The wood element makes these Dogs more open to new experiences and less judgmental. Wood Dogs can see and understand the "gray" in situations and are therefore the most empathic of all the Dog family.

FIRE DOGS • 1946, 2006 • Fire builds passion and confidence in Dogs. Fire Dogs can balance the needs of others with their own, and so are less humble and more confident than most Dogs. They are charismatic and can win support easily.

EARTH DOGS • 1958, 2018 • Double earth helps balance Dogs' anxieties and phobias. Earth Dogs are quite stable and reliable and less prone to stress than other Dogs. Earth Dogs are realistic and very practical. They are good with methodical and detailed work.

METAL DOGS • 1970 • Metal strengthens Dogs' ideals and moral beliefs. Metal Dogs like to speak their minds. They may lead chaste lives, and are far more likely than any other type of Dog to be attracted to self-sacrificing work in charities or religion.

WATER DOGS • 1922, 1982 • Water makes these Dogs more adaptable and intuitive. Water Dogs are big "softies" emotionally and are prone to taking in and caring for all the local strays. They fill their homes with unconditional love and acceptance. They are pure angels and invaluable to society.

Famous Dogs

ELVIS PRESLEY, SINGER

Presley honored his mother and remained close to his father throughout his life, which is classic behavior for all Dogs. As a Wood Dog, Elvis was empathic toward others, and deplored spending time alone. His Graceland mansion was more often than not an open house to all his family, friends, and colleagues.

SHIRLEY MACLAINE, ACTOR/WRITER

MacLaine is a classic example of a Dog in pursuit of the truth. In her books, Shirley MacLaine explains her search for and experience of a higher consciousness, and describes her theories on the meaning of life.

RELATIONSHIP CHART FOR DOGS

Dog +	Rating	Potential for harmony in love, friendship, and professional life
Tiger	Best friend	There will be much understanding and respect between these two. The practical Dog will ease the Tiger's impulsiveness, and the energetic Tiger will chase away Dog's anxieties and inner doubts.
Horse	Best friend	A solid relationship of similar temperaments and respect. Dog will understand Horse's need for freedom and will be supportive. Horse will openly demonstrate appreciation, which Dog will cherish.
Rat	Good but needs work	This pairing can work if kept at friendship level. Both signs are nagged by personal insecurities, which can accumulate with this pairing. Rat's secrecy will be misinterpreted by Dog as underhanded scheming.
Ox	Positive	Dogs and Oxen share common values, such as loyalty and respect. This pairing could work if Ox can lighten up and if Dog can maintain an understanding of Ox's temperament.
Rabbit	Good but needs work	The two have similar temperaments and are likely to put each other's needs before their own. While there will be little conflict, there will also not be much challenge between them, or much initiative taken.
Snake	Challenging	In the long run, this combination will work only with difficulty. Snake tends to be intense and secretive, and the honorable and upfront Dog is likely to see this as deceit.
Sheep	Positive	As both are very tolerant, Dog and Sheep will understand and appreciate each other's differences. Dog will generally find Sheep a moral ally. Sheep will appreciate Dog's protection.
Monkey	Challenging	Dog will be attracted to Monkey's intelligence, but will soon find Monkey devious and insincere. Monkey will be attracted to Dog's eagerness to please, but will find Dog's morals hard to abide.
Rooster	Challenging	Each has different values and beliefs. Dog will find Rooster egotistical and self-absorbed. Rooster will find Dog too moralistic and unselfish.
Dog	Good but needs work	Compassionate and caring, two Dogs could have a wonderfully fulfilling relationship, provided they throw caution to the wind on occasion and engage in some risk taking.
Pig	Positive	Pigs will be able to uplift Dogs from their worries and Dogs will find themselves cherished as faithful protectors. There will be much opportunity for success if both can avoid excessive moralizing.
Dragon	Archenemy	There will be little attraction between these two. Their moral beliefs will vary in the extreme. Egotistical Dragon will make Dog snap often, and exhausting fights will result.

DRAGON

THE POWERFUL, DYNAMIC DRAGON
1916, 1928, 1940, 1952, 1964, 1976, 1988, 2000, 2012
ENERGY: YANG
ELEMENT: EARTH
TIME: 7:00 A.M.–9:00 A.M.
MONTH: APRIL
DIRECTION: EAST/SOUTHEAST
SEASON: LATE SPRING

As the only mythical creature in the Chinese zodiac, the Dragon inspires wonder, excitement, and admiration. Dragons are colorful, confident, and vibrant in personality and win the attention and support of others with great ease.

Dragons like to participate actively in life and engage their hearts and minds fully with everything that seizes their interest. However, they are free spirits and will move on swiftly if they see something that seems more enticing. Blessed with good luck, great reserves of energy, and optimism, Dragons are skilled at leading, taking on projects few others would be prepared to undertake.

The Dragon ascendant for those born between 7:00 A.M. and 9:00 A.M.

When the Dragon is the ascendant sign, its influence will create a magnetic personality. Those with a Dragon ascendant usually display independence and confidence.

Dragons at their best Visionary, passionate, motivated, optimistic, principled, energetic, compelling, vibrant, dynamic

Dragons at their worst Demanding, dissatisfied, excessive, opinionated, intolerant, overpowering, abrupt, egocentric, unpredictable

Character traits of Dragons Dynamic, lucky, exciting, idealistic, enthusiastic, confident, vital, extravagant, energetic, physical, powerful, creative, ambitious, adventurous, brave, optimistic, intelligent

Life challenge for Dragons To learn to appreciate the benefits of patience, commitment, and inner calm.

The Dragon lover Dragons have a thirst for love and will focus a lot of energy on their intimate relationships. As lovers, they are passionate, intense, and possessive. They are both physically and emotionally demanding of their partners. Dragons love to be in love and will be so often. They are great in the heady early days of new romance, but dislike the routine and commitment necessary for long-term relationships. It is variety and the unusual that attract these feisty free spirits.

The Dragon family member Dragon children are good students and quite athletic, preferring to spend their time outdoors; they enjoy being at school if they are kept motivated. As parents, they will keep their families busy, taking regular vacations and hosting many social events. Domestic situations do not usually attract Dragons, as they suffer from claustrophobia and fear boredom. If they do finally settle down, Dragons build ultramodern homes close to nature—near oceans or on mountaintops, for example—and they will frequently redecorate.

The Dragon friend Dragons are extroverts who need lots of friends to keep them occupied and happy. They seek out exciting and interesting people who, like them, are attracted to change, mystery, and new adventures. Extremely fashion conscious, they always look good and have a wardrobe full of the newest styles. They can be counted on to magnify the good times, but can be a little unreliable during the bad. It is advisable to keep them in good spirits, as they have fiery tempers when angered.

The Dragon at work Dragons are renowned visionaries who are talented at business strategy. They command leadership positions. They require absolute control and decision-making power in any role they take on. Dragons may sometimes question their own brilliance and obvious talents and abilities; their facade of extreme confidence may sometimes cover up personal insecurities.

Ideal occupations for Dragons Visual artist, photojournalist, adventurer, athlete, business director, entrepreneur, military leader

In China, Dragons are mythical animals who live in the heavens and command the forces of nature, such as rain, wind, storms, and floods. They are viewed as awesome and volatile creatures who are fairly unpredictable. Their fifth position at Buddha's side denotes power and reverence.

The five Dragon types

WOOD DRAGONS • 1964 • The presence of wood provides Dragons with much creative talent. Wood Dragons are also renowned for their beauty, elegance, and refinement and can often be found in dominant social positions. They may also be widely admired trendsetters.

FIRE DRAGONS • 1916, 1976 • The fire element adds even more vibrancy and passion to the already quite dynamic Dragons. Fire Dragons have huge personalities and are obsessed with their social life. They are very exciting and entertaining people with generous hearts. Their only downfall is their explosive temper, which, luckily, flares only rarely.

EARTH DRAGONS • 1928, 1988 • The presence of double earth ensures that these Dragons are more grounded and emotionally balanced than others. Earth Dragons are more able than other Dragons to work as part of a team and provide wise counsel. They are lucky in that they escape the emotional torrents experienced by other Dragons; they are comfortable with who and what they are.

METAL DRAGONS • 1940, 2000 • The metal element adds strength to many of the Dragons' qualities. Metal Dragons are exhibitionistic and opinionated, and seek out positions where they will have to be noticed and heard. With their huge egos, Metal Dragons have a hard time dealing with reality and routine.

WATER DRAGONS • 1952, 2012 • The water element has these Dragons focused on others' well-being rather than their own. Water Dragons are also more diplomatic and intuitive, and they seek out positions that focus on correcting social problems. Water tends to have a calming effect; this ensures that Water Dragons do not come across too strongly with others.

Famous dragons

HAROLD ROBBINS, AUTHOR

Harold Robbins is famous for his gripping novels involving drama and intrigue. Fire Dragons have double the passion and vibrancy of other Dragons—Robbins is obviously able to channel this into his exciting epics.

EARTHA KITT, SINGER

Eartha Kitt is a more balanced Dragon who displays the classic individualistic traits for which Dragons are famous. With her stage presence and distinctive voice, Eartha Kitt won much acclaim in her role as Catwoman in the early *Batman and Robin* television series.

RELATIONSHIP CHART FOR DRAGONS

Dragon +	Rating	Potential for harmony in love, friendship, and professional life
Rat	Best friend	Both animals are charged with energy and social charisma, which will keep them satisfied. Each will be intuitive about the other's unspoken desires and will be able to meet the other's needs.
Monkey	Best friend	Dragon will be attracted to Monkey's charm and wit, and Monkey to Dragon's personal power. Monkey will be happy for Dragon to dominate, and the two will live easily together.
Ox	Challenging	A powerful combination, but one that will soon be thwarted. Ox won't be able to stand Dragon's passion for the unconventional. Dragon will quickly become bored and frustrated with Ox's fixation on routine.
Tiger	Positive	This pair will have much in common and will be able to live and work comfortably together. There is opportunity for dynamic enterprise if each learns to respect the other's time in the limelight.
Rabbit	Challenging	The magnetic and impulsive Dragon will be too much for the reserved and cautious Rabbit. Dragon will quickly tire of Rabbit's lack of strength.
Dragon	Good but needs work	A meeting of extremes, guaranteed to highlight the best and the worst in the two characters. This relationship will serve only as a personal reflection and as an opportunity for introspection.
Snake	Positive	An extremely attractive match. Dragon will feel respected and socially elevated by Snake's beauty and social graces. Snake is smart enough to appreciate Dragon's dynamic appeal.
Horse	Good but needs work	The energy and enthusiasm levels match in this pairing. Provided Dragons and Horses can agree on their goals and provide enough space for their larger-than-life personalities, a relationship will last.
Sheep	Challenging	These two are stark opposites, and it will be hard for them to find anything in common or to appreciate anything in each other. Dragon will demand adventure, while Sheep will want stability.
Rooster	Good but needs work	Mutual attraction will be assured, as both Roosters and Dragons regularly attract the limelight and share it. Unfortunately, neither one will be very interested in a committed relationship with the other.
Pig	Positive	This pairing is an example of opposites attracting. Dramatic Dragons will sweep easygoing Pigs off their feet. Pigs will reward Dragons with adoration and admiration.
Dog	Archenemy	There will be little attraction between these two. Their moral beliefs will vary greatly. Egotistical Dragon will have Dog snapping often and exhausting fights will result.

ELEMENTS AND ANIMAL TOTEM ASTROLOGY

In the Native American belief system, fire, water, air, and earth are the four elements that act as nature's forces. The four interact to ensure that living things go through a recurring process of birth, life, death, and regeneration. In animal totem astrology, each of the four seasons is governed by an element, as is each of the twelve birth times and its corresponding birth totem.

This means that each animal totem has two particular elements influencing its character and behavior at any one time. If we take the two elements and their key attributes into account when analyzing each animal totem's character, we will gain a more detailed and accurate description of that totem.

SEASONAL ELEMENTS

Just as there are recurring seasons in nature, so there are seasons to life in general. Each element governing a season of birth brings special qualities to the three animal totems for that season. These qualities relate to the animal totems' inner senses, spiritual endeavors, and general behavior.

Spring animal totems The spring animal totems, Hawk, Beaver, and Deer, have the force of fire directing their general behavior.

ELEMENT	KEY ATTRIBUTES	AREAS GOVERNED BY THE ELEMENT
Fire	Energy, passion, decisiveness, illumination, expansion	The spirit and intuition
Water	Sensitivity, flexibility, intuition, creativity, physical communication	The soul and the emotions
Earth	Stability, balance, physical patience, practicality, realism	The physical body and sensations
Air	Communication, intelligence, renewal, thought, logic	The mind and the psyche

People born during this season generally act with great energy, passion, and decisiveness. They have spirited natures and, generally, well-developed intuition.

Summer animal totems The summer animal totems, Woodpecker, Salmon, and Brown Bear, have the force of water directing their general behavior. People born during this time of the year tend to act with sensitivity toward others. They have flexible and creative natures, and their communication skills are generally well developed.

Fall animal totems The fall animal totems, Raven, Snake, and Owl, have the force of earth directing their general behavior. People born during this time generally act with patience and a great deal of realism. They have balanced and stable natures and are quite practical.

Winter animal totems The winter animal totems, Snow Goose, Otter, and Wolf, have the force of air directing their behavior. People born during this time usually show good verbal expression and logic. They have thoughtful and reflective natures and are quite intelligent.

SEASONAL TOTEMS

In the Native American astrology system, people have season totems, as well as birth totems. The season totems give us additional gifts and qualities.

Springtime animal totem: Eagle
DIRECTION: EAST / ELEMENT: FIRE

Eagles are awesome birds of prey, with tremendous strength and vitality, along with the ability to fly extremely high and far in search of prey. This is believed to give them vision and clarity about both the present and the future. Native Americans believe that eagles are messengers for the creator of the world, bringing enlightenment to the people of the earth.

People born during the spring—Hawks, Beavers, and Deer—all have the Eagle as their season totem. They are all filled with youthful vitality and have a natural interest in personal growth and development. They tend to be early risers, as they want to greet the dawn of each new day—this is the time of day when they are most productive. They represent the human lifetime of childhood and adolescence, from birth to approximately age eighteen.

Additional gifts Eagle bestows on Hawk, Beaver, and Deer:

- passion, enthusiasm, and optimism
- energy in abundance for physical activity
- clarity about present circumstances
- vision of future possibilities

The lessons Eagle brings to Hawk, Beaver, and Deer:

- the need to temper your passion and enthusiasm so you don't overwhelm others
- the need to control your energy so that it is used for worthwhile causes rather than dissipated

Summertime animal totem: Coyote

DIRECTION: SOUTH / ELEMENT: WATER

Coyotes are wild and wily animals who have so far proved adaptable to the encroachment of civilization on their natural terrain. They use their agility and sharp senses to avoid unnecessary contact with humans.

People born during summer—Woodpeckers, Salmon, and Brown Bears—all have the Coyote as their season totem. They often experience rapid growth physically, mentally, emotionally, or spiritually. They are most productive in the heat of the day—at noon—when their sharp senses can be used and their newly developed maturity well tested. They represent the human lifetime of young adulthood, from approximately eighteen to forty years old.

Additional gifts Coyote bestows on Woodpecker, Salmon, and Brown Bear:

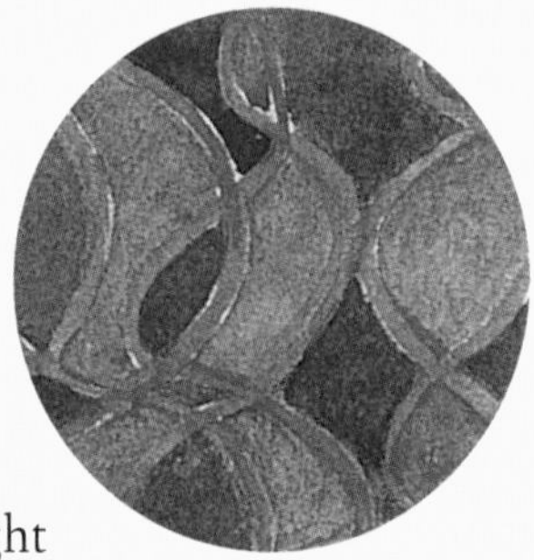

- swiftness of body and mind
- sensory acuity
- independence
- self-reliance

The lessons Coyote brings to Woodpecker, Salmon, and Brown Bear:

- the need to go in search of what feels right in order to find your calling
- the need to experience and trust in life in order to grow

Fall animal totem: Grizzly Bear

DIRECTION: WEST / ELEMENT: EARTH

Grizzly bears are enormous and powerful creatures that lead calm and mostly peaceful lives. They are slow moving, but every move is one of determination and confidence. Native Americans believe that their hibernation demonstrates their capacity for introspection, renewal, and the gaining of wisdom.

People born during the fall—Ravens, Snakes, and Owls—all have the Grizzly Bear as their season totem. Raven, Snake, and Owl people all have the capability and wisdom to hold powerful and responsible positions within the community, such as leader, healer, or teacher. They are calm and confident in any situation. They enjoy twilight—late afternoon—when they can reflect on and appraise what they have achieved during the day. They represent the human lifetime of midlife, from approximately forty to sixty years old.

Additional gifts Grizzly Bear bestows on Raven, Snake, and Owl:

- introspection and understanding of your own heart
- confidence and wisdom in any given situation
- the desire to assume responsibility for your own words and actions
- the strength to be accountable for your words and actions

The lessons Grizzly Bear brings to Raven, Snake, and Owl:

- the need to acknowledge both your strengths and your weaknesses
- the need to have a strong yet calm and controlled center, from which power will issue

Wintertime animal totem: White Buffalo

DIRECTION: NORTH / ELEMENT: AIR

The white buffalo was a rare animal, sacred to Native Americans. It would sacrifice itself for the well-being of humans. Its meat, hide, horns, and other parts were all used by Native American peoples for everything from food and clothing to shelter and weapons. The buffalo was believed to be the messenger of knowledge and to have a spiritual union with the creator of the world.

People born during winter—Snow Geese, Otters, and Wolves—all have the White Buffalo as their season totem. They are wise, independent, and people-oriented. They are highly intelligent and have active minds. As they like to take time out to rejuvenate, their best time is the night. Sleep brings them rest, and their dreams bring them powerful messages and lessons on life. They represent the human lifetime of old age, from around age sixty onward.

Additional gifts White Buffalo bestows on Snow Goose, Otter, and Wolf:

- intelligence and wisdom
- self-sacrifice and charity
- spirituality
- generosity

The lessons White Buffalo brings to Snow Goose, Otter, and Wolf:

- the need to rest and rejuvenate physically and emotionally in order to grow spiritually
- the need to keep contact with the earthly realm—to stay balanced and be realistic and practical

BIRTH TIME ELEMENTS

The element that rules each person's birth time influences the instinctive behavior of each animal totem. It is this element that creates the foundation of each animal totem's basic nature—the essence of who you are. Each of the four elements is linked with three of the twelve birth time animal totems.

Snow Goose, Beaver, and Brown Bear: EARTH

With earth as their birth time element, these animal totems all have patience and practicality at the core of their natures. They tend to operate by using their well-developed common sense. They are realistic and emotionally balanced.

Pure signs occur when the season and birth time elements are the same. In animal totem astrology, three animal totems are pure signs. These are:

• Otter—air of air

• Hawk—fire of fire

• Woodpecker—water of water

People with these totems express the attributes of their elements intensely.

Otter, Deer, and Raven: AIR

With air as their birth time element, these animal totems all have keen intellects and inquiring minds. Otter, Deer, and Raven people tend to operate using logic and rational thought. They are clever individuals with psychic abilities.

Wolf, Woodpecker, and Snake: WATER

With water as their birth time element, these animal totems are emotionally sensitive and flexible. They operate by using their usually well-developed intuition and communication skills. They are empathic and creative.

Hawk, Salmon, and Owl: FIRE

With fire as their birth time element, these animal totems are passionate and enthusiastic to the very core of their beings. They tend to operate very energetically and decisively. They are go-getters and thrive on change.

ELEMENTAL CLANS

Your elemental clan is the animal group you belong to as determined by your birth time element.

Thunderbird clan: FIRE TOTEMS—HAWK, SALMON, OWL

Like the now-extinct thunderbird, the largest and most magnificent of the hawks, and their element, Hawk, Salmon, and Owl people are powerful, radiant, and passionate. They have spirited and enthusiastic personalities and thrive on activity and change. They are charming and witty people who love being the center of attention, delighting in acknowledgment and praise from others.

Strengths to cultivate: Intuition, physical stamina, optimism, motivation

Possible weaknesses to address: Gullibility to flattery, inflated ego, oversensitivity to constructive criticism

Frog clan: WATER TOTEMS—WOLF, WOODPECKER, SNAKE

Like the frog and their element, Wolf, Woodpecker, and Snake people are very flexible and emotionally fluid individuals who possess the ability to transform themselves to suit their environments. The water element provides them with creativity and expressiveness, making them skilled communicators.

Strengths to cultivate: Empathy, communication, creativity, emotional accessibility

Possible weaknesses to address: Repression of emotions, stagnation of ideas, lack of discipline, inability to change emotional responses

Turtle clan: EARTH TOTEMS—SNOW GOOSE, BEAVER, BROWN BEAR

Like their element and their elemental animal totem, Snow Goose, Beaver, and Brown Bear people are grounded, stable, and secure. They are loyal and act according to their strong values and principles. They are very practical, constructive, and industrious.

Strengths to cultivate: Responsibility and accountability, self-sacrifice, being sensible, diligence

Possible weaknesses to address: Stubbornness, authoritative approach when dealing with others, intolerance to others' views and beliefs

Butterfly clan: AIR TOTEMS—OTTER, DEER, RAVEN

Like their elemental animal totem and element, Otter, Deer, and Raven people are beautiful to behold and delightful to have around. They are active, energetic, and ever changing, in physical appearance as well as in their feelings, thoughts, and opinions. As such, they have the power to transform and uplift those around them. They are intelligent, innovative, and expressive individuals.

Strengths to cultivate: Flexibility, spirituality, optimism, humanitarianism

Possible weaknesses to address: Lack of practicality and perseverance, lack of control in emotional responses

ELEMENTS AND THE CHINESE HOROSCOPE

EARTH YEAR
BALANCE, WISDOM, PATIENCE, PRACTICALITY

Born in an earth year: 1918, 1919, 1928, 1929, 1938, 1939, 1948, 1949, 1968, 1969, 1978, 1979, 1988, 1989, 1998, 1999, 2008, 2009, 2018, 2019

THE EARTH RAT • *Water is controlled by earth: Stability and direction.* Earth Rats are logical realists who reflect carefully before making any decisions. Full of good advice, Earth Rats rarely make a wrong move and give valuable advice to family, friends, and business associates. They appear satisfied and at peace with life's ups and downs. Years of birth: 1948, 2008

THE EARTH OX • *Double earth: Practicality and worldly wisdom.* Earth Oxen are wise, practical, and patient. They can be quite resourceful when it comes to solving problems, and often achieve their aims. Being able to engage with their emotions is their main challenge. Years of birth: 1949, 2009

THE EARTH TIGER • *Earth is utilized by wood: Core strengths harnessed.* Earth Tigers have more common sense, patience, and practicality than other Tigers. They are stable individuals who value the security of a solid foundation—a job, a home to call their own, and caring friends and family. Years of birth: 1938, 1998

THE EARTH RABBIT • *Earth is utilized by wood: Core strengths harnessed.* Traditionalist Earth Rabbits tend to be inflexible about ethics, values, and principles. They can be prudish and judgmental. They work hard for their security, which they cherish, and do not take risks. Years of birth: 1939, 1999

THE EARTH DRAGON • *Double earth: Practicality and worldly wisdom.* Earth Dragons are more sedate and calm than other Dragons. Their lives are less chaotic, as they are able to recognize and follow wise counsel. They are practical, realistic, and emotionally balanced. Years of birth: 1928, 1988

THE EARTH SNAKE • *From fire comes earth: Powerful and enhancing.* Earth Snakes are gentle souls with no hidden agendas. They radiate tranquility and calm. Their genuine care for others is demonstrated in their open communication style. They make good facilitators and counselors. Years of birth: 1929, 1989

THE EARTH HORSE • *From fire comes earth: Powerful and enhancing.* Earth Horses are able to find the stability and focus often missing in Horses' lives. They are resourceful and will apply their energy to achieving long-term goals. Earth Horses are blessed with a balance of worldly wisdom and youthful exuberance. Years of birth: 1918, 1978

THE EARTH SHEEP • *Double earth: Practicality and worldly wisdom.* Earth Sheep are focused throughout their lives on achieving spiritual fulfillment. They have a strong spiritual side. Earth Sheep are truly caring and compassionate souls, willing to sacrifice much in order to better the lives of others. Years of birth: 1919, 1979

THE EARTH MONKEY • *From earth comes metal: Engaging and activating.* Earth Monkeys are more interested in lending their mental dexterity to useful pursuits than to fun and games. They are interested in lifelong learning, taking evening classes and acquiring many qualifications. Years of birth: 1968, 2028

THE EARTH ROOSTER • *From earth comes metal: Engaging and activating.* Earth provides the usually flamboyant Roosters with much-needed reserve in both dress and communication style. Earth Roosters do not avoid accountability. They are practical and grounded, full of common sense and responsibility. Years of birth: 1969, 2029

THE EARTH DOG • *Double earth: Emphasis on balance and worldly wisdom.* Earth emphasizes these Dogs' reliability and steadfast devotion, and ensures that they do not fall prey to depression and self-doubt. Earth Dogs are therefore more able to take negative blows. They take their commitments seriously. Years of birth: 1958, 2018

THE EARTH PIG • *Water is controlled by earth: A grounded quality and a sense of direction.* Earth Pigs make natural homemakers. They desire security and do not value careers, travel, or an adventurous life. Earth Pigs are happiest when they are married, have children, and are comfortably settled in their family home. They take great pleasure in the daily routines of family life. Years of birth: 1959, 2019

FIRE YEAR
PASSION, ENERGY, DECISIVENESS, ENTHUSIASM

Born in a fire year: 1916, 1917, 1926, 1927, 1936, 1937, 1966, 1967, 1976, 1977, 1986, 1987, 1996, 1997, 2006, 2007, 2016, 2017

THE FIRE RAT • *Fire is controlled by water: Opportunity to control the darker side.* Fire Rats are always on the go both physically and mentally, finding it hard to slow down or even take a rest. Fire Rats are more forthright and passionately outspoken than other Rats, and do not usually suffer from this sign's inclination toward stress and anxiety. Years of birth: 1936, 1996

THE FIRE OX • *From fire comes earth: Powerfully enhancing.* This is one Ox you want as a friend, not as an enemy. Fire Oxen have volatile personalities and can pack quite a force both physically and verbally when challenged or confronted. For all their huff and puff, they are also full of enthusiasm and passion. Years of birth: 1937, 1997

THE FIRE TIGER • *From wood comes fire: Passion and energy.* Fire Tigers exhibit enormous energy and magnetism. They are courageous, taking unthinkable risks. Fire Tigers pack a lot of activity and adventure into their lives and want constant change in their careers and relationships. Years of birth: 1926, 1986

THE FIRE RABBIT • *From wood comes fire: Passion and energy.* Gusto, courage, and motivation are just what Rabbits require to really get going. Fire Rabbits are the most successful Rabbits in high-profile professions. They are able to blend intuition and reflection with personal magnetism and are often hugely popular individuals. Years of birth: 1927, 1987

THE FIRE DRAGON • *From fire comes earth: Powerfully enhancing.* Fire Dragons appear like bolts of lightning—magnetic, magnificent, energizing, and awe-inspiring. They are totally aware of their effect on others and take pleasure in it. Their life is full of dazzling social engagements, interesting people, and exciting places. Years of birth: 1916, 1976

THE FIRE SNAKE • *Double fire: Energy and dynamism.* Double fire gives Snakes all the physical resources they require to match their superior intellects. Fire Snakes are unstoppable in business and will achieve high status quickly and with ease. Years of birth: 1917, 1977

THE FIRE HORSE • *Double fire: Energy and dynamism.* Double fire blows the energy meters off Horses. They are hurried, daring, and restless. Fire Horses have numerous projects on the go at one time and find it hard to concentrate on detail or to take a methodical approach. They will also find commitment difficult; they are more comfortable single. Years of birth: 1966, 2026

THE FIRE SHEEP • *From fire comes earth: Powerfully enhancing.* Fire Sheep have the willpower and motivation to achieve their goals. Unlike other Sheep, who are more idle and placid, Fire Sheep are confident and have a warm, caring, and winning personality. Fire Sheep make appealing socialites and good networkers. Year of birth: 1967

THE FIRE MONKEY • *Metal is molded by fire: Intensity and direction.* Fire Monkeys are focused on power and control from an early age. Theirs is not a personality given to compassion and a sense of fair play. They can be ruthless and have flexible values and principles if necessary. Years of birth: 1956, 2016

THE FIRE ROOSTER • *Metal is molded by fire: Intensity and direction.* Fire Roosters are bold, direct, and blunt. They can appear extremely loud and colorful. Fire Roosters like to make dramatic entrances, parade across grand dance floors, and generally be the focus of attention. Years of birth: 1957, 2017

THE FIRE DOG • *From fire comes earth: Powerful and enhancing.* Fire Dogs do not lose sight of their own needs and desires the way other Dog types can. They are passionate about humanitarian causes and quietly confident in their ability to make a real difference. They require little effort to win others' support, and

generally lead a comfortable, emotionally fulfilled life. Years of birth: 1946, 2006

THE FIRE PIG • *Fire is controlled by water: Action.* Fire Pigs are proactive, confident, and motivated enough to aim for specific goals. They can be too keen to win others' approval, which can lead to danger. They need to practice more patience to ensure their own safety. Years of birth: 1947, 2007

METAL YEAR
TENACITY, DETERMINATION, RESILIENCE, PHYSICAL STRENGTH
Born in a metal year: 1920, 1921, 1930, 1931, 1940, 1941, 1950, 1951, 1960, 1961, 1970, 1971, 1980, 1981, 1990, 1991, 2000, 2001, 2010, 2011

THE METAL RAT • *From metal comes water: Strength and structure.* Metal gives Rats mental and physical strength. Metal Rats have strong opinions and need to voice them often. This can make them appear stubborn and inflexible; however, they balance this with supreme efficiency. Years of birth: 1900, 1960

THE METAL OX • *From earth comes metal: Engaging and activating.* Metal adds even more physical strength and mental willpower to Oxen. Metal Oxen know exactly what they want and do not waste time. Not usually affectionate by nature, they balance this by being reliable providers. Years of birth: 1901, 1961

THE METAL TIGER • *Wood is controlled by metal: Strength and domination.* Metal Tigers are extremely passionate and volatile, and occasionally overbearing. Loaded with confidence and energy, they are usually quite ambitious and ruthless in business dealings. They demonstrate little of the Tiger's usual easy rapport with others. Years of birth: 1950, 2010

THE METAL RABBIT • *Wood is controlled by metal: Strength and domination.* Metal gives Rabbits the perseverance and bravery they usually lack. Metal Rabbits are likely to be detached from their emotions when making decisions. They are cunning and manipulative in business affairs. Years of birth: 1951, 2011

THE METAL DRAGON • *From earth comes metal: Engaging and activating.* The metal element intensifies Dragons' magnetic and strong-willed personality. With an abundance of confidence and self-appreciation, Metal Dragons do not easily accept defeat or failure. Years of birth: 1940, 2000

THE METAL SNAKE • *Metal is molded by fire: Skillful.* Metal Snakes are too calculating and discriminating for their own good. They want the best life can offer and will set out with cool logic and detachment to find a position of influence and power. Years of birth: 1941, 2001

THE METAL HORSE • *Metal is molded by fire: Energizing.* Metal Horses are always on the go. Headstrong and hard to tame, they find it impossible to adapt to routine. Metal Horses are addicted to freedom, open spaces, and constant change. Their boldness and engaging personalities add to their sexual appeal. When focused, they can be quite productive. Years of birth: 1930, 1990

THE METAL SHEEP • *From earth comes metal: Engaging and activating.* Metal Sheep have stronger characters than other Sheep. They are able to adjust their sensitivities to gain more of what they want from others. Once sure of their foundations, they will embark on a quest for beauty. Years of birth: 1931, 1991

THE METAL MONKEY • *Double metal: Intellectual pursuits.* Double metal increases Monkeys' intellectual and physical abilities. Metal Monkeys rarely rely on others for assistance. They respect money, and will rarely take uncalculated risks with it. In social settings they appear lively, witty, passionate, and convincing. Years of birth: 1920, 1980

THE METAL ROOSTER • *Double metal: Intellectual rigor.* Double metal makes Roosters extremely industrious. They are passionate about their careers and demonstrate a flair for investigation, practicality, and detailed decision making. They can be uncompromising when dealing with others, expecting excellence. Years of birth: 1921, 1981

THE METAL DOG • *From earth comes metal: Engaging and activating.* Metal Dogs are stern idealists. They are serious and directed individuals, particularly when it comes to questions of morality and justice. Metal Dogs often devote themselves to worthy causes. Years of birth: 1910, 1970

THE METAL PIG • *From metal comes water: Strength and structure.* Metal Pigs have big appetites for all the pleasures in life. Unlike other Pigs, they work hard to acquire their wants. Extroverted, affectionate, and openly demonstrative, Metal Pigs appeal to the opposite sex and can successfully balance the work, fun, and love in their life. Years of birth: 1911, 1971

WATER YEAR

SENSITIVITY, COMMUNICATION SKILLS, INTUITION, CREATIVITY
Born in a water year: 1912, 1913, 1922, 1923, 1932, 1933, 1942, 1943, 1952, 1953, 1962, 1963, 1972, 1973, 1982, 1983, 1992, 1993, 2002, 2003, 2012, 2013

THE WATER RAT • *Double water: Intuition, communication, and emotions.* Double water lends Rats a natural eloquence, leading them into communication-centered careers such as public speaking or professional writing. Years of birth: 1912, 1972

THE WATER OX • *Water controlled by earth: Emotional accessibility.* Just what Oxen need—access to their emotional side. Water Oxen are softer and more approachable than other Oxen. Empathic and considerate, they are still very practical. Years of birth: 1913, 1973

THE WATER TIGER • *From water grows wood: An enhancing combination.* Water makes Tigers quieter and more carefree. Water Tigers are highly intuitive. Socially, they have an extroverted, optimistic presence. Water Tigers are sensitive to others' needs. Years of birth: 1902, 1962

THE WATER RABBIT • *From water grows wood: An enhancing combination.* Water Rabbits are supersensitive, acutely aware of

themselves in all environments. This can create a neurotic, inwardly focused personality. Years of birth: 1903, 1963

THE WATER DRAGON • *Water is directed by earth: Empathy and intuition.* Dragons need a dose of water to soften their exuberant personalities and occasionally shift their focus from themselves. Water Dragons are far more considerate and caring than other Dragons. Years of birth: 1952, 2012

THE WATER SNAKE • *Fire is controlled by water: Clarity and intuition.* Water Snakes are amazingly gifted—the embodiment of intuitive perception. With their keen sensory acuity, little passes them by. Water Snakes are often found in "spiritual" professions, where they can use their gifts to see beyond the obvious. Years of birth: 1953, 2013

THE WATER HORSE • *Fire is controlled by water: Intuition and mental creativity*. Water Horses are less focused on the physical world and more focused on their natural creative and/or communication skills. They are often gifted orators, able to build a story to an emotional finale. Years of birth: 1942, 2002

THE WATER SHEEP • *Water is controlled by earth: Emotions and intuition.* Water Sheep engage with life emotionally, rarely using logic or reflection for objectivity. They are easily wounded by criticism and extremely sensitive to their surroundings, and their mental and physical health is accordingly delicate. Years of birth: 1943, 2003

THE WATER MONKEY • *From metal comes water: Empathy and reflection.* Water ensures that Monkeys are not too quick to trifle with others' feelings. Water Monkeys demonstrate empathy and will use their keen intellects to solve problems rather than create them. They are oriented more toward the group than toward themselves as individuals. Years of birth: 1932, 1992

THE WATER ROOSTER • *From metal comes water: Empathy and intuition.* Water Roosters are softer and more flexible than other Roosters. They use their intuition to avoid being too direct with others. With their appealing combination of self-awareness, flamboyance, and understanding of others, they are naturally the focus of attention. Years of birth: 1933, 1993

THE WATER DOG • *From metal comes water: Empathy*. Water Dogs are more reflective and adaptable than other Dogs. They are more lenient on themselves and others, and will allow for much fun and frivolity in their lives. They will also fall for any hard-luck story. Water Dogs are popular with others and will never want for love, friendship, or support. Years of birth: 1922, 1982

THE WATER PIG • *Double water: Intuition, communication, and emotions.* Double water intensifies the already emotionally charged personality of most Pigs, making Water Pigs supersensitive to others and overly indulgent. Increasingly introspective with age and experience, Water Pigs' ability to deal with hardships in life can quickly diminish. They will often need the help of others in order to escape their plight. Years of birth: 1923, 1983

WOOD YEAR

RESOURCEFULNESS, CREATIVITY, SPIRITUAL GROWTH, OPTIMISM

Born in a wood year: 1914, 1915, 1924, 1925, 1934, 1935, 1944, 1945, 1954, 1955, 1964, 1965, 1974, 1975, 1984, 1985, 1994, 1995, 2004, 2005, 2014, 2015

THE WOOD RAT • *From water grows wood: An enhancing combination.* Wood Rats display more creative talent and interest in spirituality than other Rats. Their optimism and heightened

resourcefulness overcome much of Rats' usual worries about security, and this frees them to indulge a little in their passions. Wood Rats are caring, empathic, and popular. Years of birth: 1924, 1984

THE WOOD OX • *Earth is controlled by wood: Harnessed strengths.* Wood Oxen are dependable, stable, clear of purpose, and rigidly adhere to their principles and values. Highly ethical, they avoid the lightweight and lighthearted. They tend to follow a traditional path, enjoying the comfort and security of a home and family. Years of birth: 1925, 1985

THE WOOD TIGER • *Double wood: Expansion and personal growth.* Double wood gives Tigers twice as much gaiety and childlike enthusiasm. Wood Tigers are irrepressible and will often be surrounded by an adoring crowd. They detest commitment in all forms, preferring to spend their time traveling, exploring, learning, and generally experiencing all that life has to offer. Years of birth: 1914, 1974

THE WOOD RABBIT • *Double wood: Expansion and personal growth.* Wood Rabbits are usually artistically talented and have creative occupations. They are quite generous and give freely of themselves. While eager for financial wealth, they are quick spenders, particularly when it comes to traveling in search of inspiration. Years of birth: 1915, 1975

THE WOOD DRAGON • *Earth is utilized by wood: Harnessed strengths.* Wood Dragons are generally creative, engaging, and beautiful to behold, full of elegance, style, and refined taste. As such, they are naturals in the highest social circles. They usually marry well and spend their time directing public charity events. Years of birth: 1964, 2024

THE WOOD SNAKE • *Wood fuels fire: Sensuality and sexuality.* Wood Snakes may give in to laziness and indulgence in sensual delights rather than accomplishing anything outside their own needs. Career, power, and influence are not as important to Wood Snakes as they are to other Snakes, so they can fall far short of their true potential. Years of birth: 1965, 2025

THE WOOD HORSE • *Fire is controlled by water: Recklessness tamed.* Wood Horses are more relaxed and less excitable than other Horses. They demonstrate stability in all facets of life, from romance to career. Wood Horses are cooperative and caring, yet tend to be gullible. Years of birth: 1954, 2014

THE WOOD SHEEP • *Earth controls wood: Stability and direction.* Wood Sheep are extremely creative and artistic. Unmotivated by money or fame, they spend all their time on creative and artistic pursuits. Generous to a fault, Wood Sheep are also compassionate and caring. Years of birth: 1955, 2015

THE WOOD MONKEY • *Wood is controlled by metal: Strength and domination.* Wood Monkeys are more balanced and less volatile than other Monkeys, with a methodical approach to solving problems. They are more capable of specific achievements and less attracted to practical jokes than other Monkeys. Years of birth: 1944, 2004

THE WOOD ROOSTER • *Wood is controlled by metal: Expansion.* Wood Roosters show an early interest in personal growth and take every opportunity to challenge their own beliefs and explore other options. They are keen seekers of knowledge, and their homes are full of half-read books. Wood Roosters are more flexible and adaptable than other Roosters. Years of birth: 1945, 2005

THE WOOD DOG • *Earth is utilized by wood: Personal growth.* Wood Dogs are more fun loving and optimistic than other Dogs. They are open to life's experiences, willing to change their values and principles. Wood Dogs are deeply empathetic and place fewer expectations on themselves than other Dogs tend to do. Years of birth: 1934, 1994

THE WOOD PIG • *From water grows wood: An enhancing combination.* Wood gives Pigs the opportunity for total self-expression. Wood Pigs can talk and talk and talk. They need to consider careers where their verbal talents can be appreciated. Sometimes Wood Pigs can be too quick to express their opinions—they need to be careful to avoid giving offense. Years of birth: 1935, 1955

F

FEBRUARY

FEBRUARY ~ AQUARIUS
FROM THE 1ST TO THE 18TH

This second segment of the air sign of Aquarius suggests a talent for arbitration and communication and the courage to stick to your guns. The Chinese sign of the active Wood Tiger is responsible for your sparkling personality, magnetic looks, and sense of humor. The active wood element encourages you to make a success out of your own interests, but it is hard for you to work for others.

The Vedic sign of Makara brings you down to earth, as it adds common sense and a practical attitude; the Uttara Bhadra mansion lends the ability to talk persuasively and to take on challenges with courage and fortitude. If you were born under the Revati mansion, you will be a good organizer who can achieve success after a struggle, and you can expect to travel far.

The Native American Otter of the Butterfly clan ensures that you are logical, humorous, and fun to be with. You make a sympathetic friend and a respected and honored boss. In West Africa, the authoritative and humanitarian Baobab Tree starts the month, but it soon changes to the sign of the Wealth of Amber and Silver, which gives you strong emotions and an inventive mind. This also enhances your counseling abilities.

The month starts with the Celtic tree symbol of the Cypress,

which ensures good looks and a slightly aristocratic manner, but it soon changes to the Poplar, which emphasizes being concerned about others. Then the dynamic Cedar comes in, adding enterprise and magnetism. In matters of love you can be overly sensitive. The Runic sign of Algiz allows you to get away with things that would defeat others, but this is soon followed by the headstrong sign of Sowelo, which makes it hard for you to admit to faults.

FEBRUARY ~ PISCES
FROM THE 19TH ONWARD

The gentle, creative water sign of Pisces means that you love going out and meeting interesting people. You are a sucker for a hard-luck story, and you can waste years rescuing others or fulfilling their needs while neglecting your own. However, the Chinese Tiger gives you just the touch of rebellion and ambition that saves you from being a wimp. The active wood element adds to your idealism—it makes you trustworthy, and it also makes you astute and realistic.

Your Vedic sign starts out as the practical and ambitious Makara, but soon changes to the inventive and exciting sign of Kumbha, which brings a little much-needed obstinacy. Both these mansions help prevent your heart from totally ruling your head. The Revati mansion gives you organizing ability and encourages you to travel, but this soon changes to Ashwini, which makes you bold and outspoken.

The Native Americans see you as a Cougar of the Frog clan, which gives you a mystical spirit and healing ability. You can shut your feelings away when you are hurt, and there is some loneliness about you, but this may actually be an aid to your clairvoyant abilities. West Africans see you as belonging to the Wealth of Amber and Silver, which indicates that your emotions run deep and that you need personal space. Your understanding of human nature makes you an excellent counselor.

The Celtic Pine Tree makes you a perfectionist, and far more interested in your appearance than most Pisceans, while the Norse symbol of Sowelo gives you the ability to think and act at speed. The following Norse symbol, Tiwaz, suggests strength of mind and a talent for legal argument. You keep your promises.

FENG SHUI AND CHINESE ASTROLOGY

Feng shui specialists aim to maximize the energy flow throughout every space in a person's environment. They do this by carefully considering such things as the direction, shape, and color of houses, gardens, rooms, doors, windows, and furnishings, and suggesting useful changes or additions. Knowledge of your dominant animal sign and corresponding element (see pages 17–21), and whether your animal sign is yin or yang, will assist feng shui specialists in making appropriate recommendations for you.

The basis of Chinese astrology and feng shui is the concept of energy, or *qi*. The Chinese believe that all matter on earth—living creatures and empty space alike—is comprised of qi, which takes one of two forms, yang or yin. Yang energy is "masculine"—or positive—and is manifested as extroversion in the personality. The yang, or active energy, rules the masculine characteristics of assertion, drive, ambition, originality, and the will to fight. Yin energy, in contrast, is "feminine"—or negative—and is manifested as introversion in the personality. The yin, or receptive energy, rules the feminine characteristics of nurturing, conserving, protecting, enduring, and continuing.

The two forms of energy are opposites, but they are interdependent. If you consider warriors or inventors on one hand, and farmers and homemakers on the other, you will see how both yang and yin are necessary for humanity to change and progress (yang) and to continue and conserve (yin).

The concept of yin/yang energy plays a central role in determining some common traits of, and potential for compatibility between, the twelve animal signs. Each of the twelve animals in Chinese astrology exhibits either yang or yin energy. This is the initial basis for differentiating between the animals and for determining their potential compatibility or conflict with others.

BALANCING YIN AND YANG ENERGY

Yang animals—the Rat, Tiger, Dragon, Monkey, Horse, and Dog— are the more naturally extroverted and physically active animals. They require specific yin-oriented features in their environment to promote rest, reflection, and rejuvenation.

Yin animals—the Ox, Rabbit, Snake, Sheep, Rooster, and Pig—are the more naturally introverted and physically passive animals. They require specific yang-oriented features in their environment to build their energy reserves and promote more activity.

Sample yin features for yang animals Dark, wet, soft, cold, down, north, inward, receptive, curvy, round

Sample yang features for yin animals Light, dry, hard, warm/hot, up, south, outward, creative, straight, angular

Providing harmony through the elements Note your primary element, and also your dominant element, based on your year of birth (see the Chinese Year Chart, pages 19–21).

The table below details some specific features identified with each element. By applying the features of your primary and dominant element(s) to your environment, you can promote a feeling of personal well-being.

The elements flow in cycles, which can be either productive or destructive. In the productive cycle, the earth produces metal, metal contains water, water replenishes wood, wood helps fuel a fire, and fire aids earth. In the destructive cycle, earth muddies water, water quenches fire, fire melts metal, metal chops wood, and wood depletes the earth.

The productive cycle: wood, fire, earth, metal, water
Those who have a double element, i.e., where the primary and dominant elements are the same, need to reduce this buildup by applying the features of the element that can destroy it.

The destructive cycle: wood, earth, water, fire, metal
You can use the elements to balance the energies so that they are productive rather than destructive. For instance, if you have a primary element of earth and a dominant element of water—a combination that is usually considered destructive—include aspects of metal in your environment to help rebalance this dynamic.

FEATURE	WOOD	FIRE	EARTH	METAL	WATER
Direction	East	South	Midpoint	West	North
Color	Green	Red	Yellow	White	Black
Season	Spring	Summer	All	Fall	Winter
Shape	Tall/columnar	Pointed/triangular	Flat/low	Round	Undulating/irregular
Energy	Outward	Upward	Horizontal	Inward	Downward

G

GEMINI

MAY 22 TO JUNE 21
SYMBOL: THE TWINS
RULING PLANET: MERCURY
GROUPS: POSITIVE, AIR, MUTABLE

You often want two things at once and need constant stimulation to keep you interested in long-term projects. Like the element that governs your Sun sign, you are breezy in character. You are able to communicate exceptionally well and you are usually renowned for your wit. Your challenge is to keep yourself from being bored; you find it difficult to finish long-term projects and need to train yourself to persevere to the end of a task.

You need the stability of a happy relationship, a regular job, and a settled home, but you also need variety. You usually have a short attention span and do not suffer fools gladly. You tend to be impatient with those who are not as clever as you. As Geminis hate boredom, their constant search for something more makes them appear changeable or as if they have multiple personalities. Geminis need to develop a strong sense of compassion and tolerance— otherwise they will find themselves with few friends.

You usually find your way into a job that puts you into contact with many people and gives you a variety of different tasks to do during the course of the day. One famous Gemini was John F. Kennedy. You can often appear confident and charming while

---

ASTROLOGICAL COMPATIBILITY

WHAT SUN SIGN ARE YOU? Gemini
WHO ARE YOUR FRIENDS? Aries, Leo
WHO ARE YOUR LOVERS? Taurus, Virgo

feeling insecure and unloved. This sense of insecurity can sometimes lead to your feeling fragmented and deeply unhappy. Use your powerful intellect to realize that you are a complex person who needs to balance your many sides.

Geminis are attracted to jobs that are inherently varied and that allow them to communicate and be seen. Acting is an attractive career option for a Gemini—famous Geminis include a number of talented, mercurial actors, such as Marilyn Monroe and Errol Flynn.

Geminis love language—famous Geminis also include authors and songwriters, such as Sir Arthur Conan Doyle and Bob Dylan. Geminis enjoy exercising their considerable intellectual skills. They are often very quick and clever, usually displaying a great sense of humor; this often comes through in their art or work.

Worrying about relatively unimportant matters is your weakness, and you can get on your own nerves as well as others'. Another challenge is to avoid simply looking at the surface of things and to develop a deeper interest in or appreciation of a job or a relationship.

You like buying good clothes, and you are unlikely to live in untidy or uncomfortable surroundings. You have a strong sense of style and culture, loving things that are beautiful or interesting. You are generally slim and tall, almost willowy, and you are able to retain your youthful appearance and attitudes for many years.

■ FOR **GOAT** (CHINESE ASTROLOGY), SEE **SHEEP** ON PAGES 160–63.

H

■ FOR **HARE** (CHINESE ASTROLOGY),
SEE **RABBIT** ON PAGES 138–41.

HAWK

Native Americans believe that hawks are messengers of the sky. Sighting one or hearing its cry is an omen of new arrivals or new things about to happen, either good or bad. So seeing or hearing a hawk signals the need to become more aware of the environment and to be prepared for change. Hawk people are often seen as the messengers of insight and the seekers of truth, demonstrating keen perceptiveness and foresight about their own daily lives as well as about the lives of others. Nothing escapes their X-ray vision; nothing can quench their determination to uncover the truth in all matters.

Hawks are "big-picture" people who need to see the overall plan before they can attend to minute details. However, once they are committed to an overall plan, Hawks can easily apply their acute perception to even minor aspects to ensure no details are ignored.

SEASON	Early spring—a time of birth, of new life and budding, and of awakening from winter's hibernation
SEASON TOTEM	Eagle
SEASON ELEMENT	Fire
BIRTH TIME	March 21–April 19 Northern Hemisphere September 23–October 22 Southern Hemisphere
BIRTH TIME ELEMENT	Fire
ELEMENTAL CLAN	Thunderbird
ENERGY FLOW	Active
AFFINITIES	Color: yellow Plant: dandelion Mineral: opal
GIFTS	Foresight, energy, optimism, perceptiveness, boldness, honesty, sincerity, independence
CHALLENGES	Rashness, willfulness, impatience, impulsiveness
LIFE PATH	To pace oneself in everyday life and reflect more on the likely outcomes of one's actions before starting anything.

Action-oriented, bold, and quick, given their active energy-flow type, Hawks would rather initiate new ideas and projects than attend to their completion. Once things are up and running, they prefer to lead others, getting them to attend to routine activities and completion. Hawks often fly from one project to another quite quickly, as this suits their lightning-fast minds and physical momentum. However, as this swift energy comes only in short bursts, long-range projects are best avoided. Hawks readily and quite naturally embrace change.

IDEAL PAIRINGS	
Hawk +	Relationship potential
Salmon	Both have high energy. Hawk will provide the ideas and foresight, while Salmon will provide the determination necessary for enacting all plans.
Owl	Both have a strong sense of right and wrong. They will find their values match and will be happy to live according to their principles.
Otter	Both are quite active and optimistic individuals. Their energies will easily match, and each will strengthen the other.
Deer	Hawk will provide Deer with boldness and foresight, while Deer will encourage Hawk's gentler side.
Raven	**Complement.** A natural attraction and kinship exists between these two animal totems. Each will make the other a loyal and supportive companion.

CHALLENGING PAIRINGS	
Hawk +	Relationship potential
Snow Goose	Snow Goose will grow increasingly frustrated with Hawk's impatience. Hawk will find Snow Goose too stubborn and unwilling to change.
Beaver	Steadfast Beaver will come into the relationship with set opinions. Hawk will want to take a more liberal approach. They will soon part.
Woodpecker	These two operate at different levels. Hawks are bold and independent, while Woodpeckers are introverted and dependent. Neither will have their needs met in this relationship.
Brown Bear	Impulsive Hawk will find the methodical Brown Bear stodgy and stifling. Brown Bear will soon be openly criticizing Hawk's impulsive behavior.
Snake	Snake is patient, while Hawk is rash. Neither will be able to understand the other's behavior. They will soon part to find more compatible companions.
Wolf	Hawk is impatient and impulsive, while Wolf is restless and indecisive. Neither will be able to make a decision that will make both happy.
Hawk	Hawk pairing with another will bring about a mirroring effect, whereby the best and the worst in each other will be magnified.

HORSE

THE VITAL, AGILE HORSE
1918, 1930, 1942, 1954, 1966, 1978, 1990, 2002, 2014
ENERGY: YANG
ELEMENT: FIRE
TIME: 11:00 A.M.–1:00 P.M.
MONTH: JUNE
DIRECTION: SOUTH
SEASON: SUMMER

Horses are the restless adventurers of the Chinese zodiac.
Energetic and active, they are constantly on the move. They take up
causes eagerly and impetuously. They like to live independent lives
and to be free to roam and explore all areas of life. They are afraid
of being trapped in any situation and want to live without having to
commit themselves long-term to any person, object, or goal.

Optimistic, upbeat, and energetic, Horses are keenly sought after
as friends and personal coaches. They love to socialize and to be the
focus of attention. They often maintain their good health and
youthful appearance far longer than others.

The Horse ascendant for those born between 11:00 A.M. and
1:00 P.M.

The Horse as the ascendant sign adds vitality and physical agility.
Those with Horse ascendants can also become restless and may be
bored easily.

Horses at their best Independent, deft, enthusiastic, youthful,
frank, gregarious, enterprising, energetic, generous, chatty, brave

Horses at their worst Temperamental, impatient, hot-tempered,
irresponsible, opportunistic, unscrupulous

Character traits of Horses Independent, headstrong, ambitious,

Horse's seventh position at Buddha's side represents youthful
vitality and freedom. People born in Horse years are by nature
quite active, adventurous, restless, and young at heart. Horse
people have so much excess energy that they will continually
involve themselves in daredevil outdoor and sporty pursuits in
the vain hope of tiring themselves out. Horses are the Chinese
zodiac's absolute free spirits. If their freedom is hindered in any
way, they may be prone to bouts of claustrophobia.

hardworking, talkative, energetic, dexterous, sociable, strong, bold, intelligent, confident, brave, opportunistic, competitive, youthful

Life challenge for Horses To integrate quiet thought, reflection, focus, and tenacity into their daily lives.

The Horse lover Most Horses are physically attractive and will remain so for much of their lives. Their charisma and energy act like a magnet. Horses are physically exhausting as lovers! Horses love a challenge and will throw themselves into the game of love with abandon and zest. Dashing and daring, Horses excel as heroic lovers who come galloping in to rescue their fair damsels or handsome males from less attractive suitors. Unfortunately, their persistent restlessness and attraction to greener pastures will have them quickly moving on to other, unexplored terrain. Horse affairs are always short—but memorable.

The Horse family member It is rare for Horses to settle down; the only way to achieve this is if their partners offer much adoration, praise, and understanding. Horses detest jealousy and their partners will need to learn quickly to give them plenty of room in the relationship.

Once settled, Horses make good protectors of their families and revel in their children's company. Horses are dexterous and are likely to build their family homes, along with much of the furniture, single-handed. Provided they are kept challenged and interested professionally, they can make steady and generous providers.

The Horse friend There's no such thing as a quiet, intimate get-together when a Horse is involved. Even during a quick chat over coffee, Horses will dominate the conversation—they may also try to coax you into a brisk walk. Horses love company, but will set the pace in all shared activities. Horse friends are cheery and optimistic and will do their best to rouse others from their doldrums. On a whim they will suggest all manner of things to do and will expect their pals to jump with enthusiasm. Horses make good protectors of their friends.

The Horse at work Horses are best in frontline, people-oriented positions where they can use their extensive interpersonal skills to the fullest. They are advised to seek mobile, outdoor positions that

will challenge them and keep them on the move in a variety of
environments. Their manual skills can also earn them a good
living—hence building, cabinetmaking, or craftwork may suit
them. If restlessness persists, anything in the travel industry will
keep them happily occupied.

Ideal occupations for Horses Photographer, salesperson,
technician, builder, jockey, race-car driver, tour operator

The five Horse types

WOOD HORSES • 1954, 2014 • Wood helps balance the emotions of
the volatile Horse, ensuring that Wood Horses appear more calm
and relaxed with themselves and with others. Emotionally stable
Wood Horses find it easier than other Horses to settle down and
commit to long-range plans.

FIRE HORSES • 1966 • Double fire means these Horses are even
more passionate and frantic daredevils than the other types. It is
impossible to tame Fire Horses and have them commit to any plan
or relationship. They are true free spirits, destined to travel the
planet unhindered.

EARTH HORSES • 1918, 1978 • The earth element provides these
Horses with much-needed stability and resourcefulness. Earth
Horses are more serious and determined than others, and more
likely to accomplish everything they set out to achieve in life.

METAL HORSES • 1930, 1990 • Metal provides Horses with more
tenacity and resolution. Metal Horses are headstrong, with volatile
emotions. To keep them happy, they need to be given a lot of
freedom, motivation, and praise in their relationships as well as
in their work.

WATER HORSES • 1942, 2002 • Water strengthens Horses'
communication skills and artistic ability. Water Horses make
entertaining storytellers and imaginative artists, and require more
freedom of expression and speech than they do physical space.

Famous horses

SEAN CONNERY, ACTOR

Sean Connery displays all the youthful vitality and dexterity for
which Horses are famous, and also the typical headstrong resolute
traits that are specific to Metal Horses. A versatile actor who, like
all Horses, has aged gracefully, Connery has appealed to all in his
heroic, action-packed movies.

RELATIONSHIP CHART FOR HORSES

Horse +	Rating	Potential for harmony in love, friendship, and professional life
Tiger	Best friend	A beneficial pairing, where each will be able to provide the other with the freedom and fanfare craved. Horses will encourage Tigers to pursue their dreams, and Tigers will reward Horses with lots of excitement.
Dog	Best friend	A solid relationship, based on similar temperaments and mutual respect. Dogs will understand Horses' need for freedom and will be supportive. Horses will openly demonstrate their appreciation, which Dogs will cherish.
Ox	Challenging	A mutual lack of understanding and respect will unfold quickly with this pairing. Horse will crave freedom and excitement and will soon leave the traditional and authoritative Ox.
Rabbit	Challenging	Much frustration and misunderstanding will mark this pairing. Energetic and fiery Horse will lose patience with the steady pace and passivity of Rabbit.
Dragon	Good but needs work	The energy and enthusiasm levels will match in this pairing. Provided Dragon and Horse can agree on their goals and have enough space for each other's larger-than-life personality, the relationship will last.
Snake	Challenging	A case of opposites attracting at first sight. Snake will be impressed with Horse's free spirit, and Horse will be attracted to Snake's charm. They will soon find little else to appreciate.
Horse	Good but needs work	Provided neither asks for commitment from the other, these two spirited adventurers will end up traveling the world together. Both are reckless, which may lead to drama along the way.
Sheep	Positive	These two will have much in common, especially creative ability, which they will encourage and help to develop in the other. The only hurdle will be Horse's lack of commitment.
Monkey	Good but needs work	Each will be attracted to the other's energy and enthusiasm. However, Horses wear their hearts on their sleeves, and can be a little gullible, which secretive Monkeys will not appreciate.
Rooster	Good but needs work	Both are lively and entertaining, which will ensure an initial attraction. However, Rooster will want to control the relationship, which will cause Horse to bolt.
Pig	Positive	This couple will be popular and will have an active social life together. At some point Horse will want to travel abroad, and Pig will want to stay at home.
Rat	Archenemy	Both have healthy egos, which will be bruised regularly in this pairing. Horse will want physical and verbal freedom, which the politically correct Rat will be loath to respect.

JANUARY

JANUARY ~ CAPRICORN
FROM THE 1ST TO THE 19TH

The earth sign of Capricorn makes you practical, sensible, ambitious, and good to your family. You are less cautious and more interested in art and literature than the December Capricorns. Your Chinese Ox sign makes you a home-lover with a need for comfort and the good things of life. You are practical and thorough, and you work hard because you fear poverty. The receptive earth element

ensures that you are capable and efficient, but with an eye for what looks good and what works. Earth people in both these traditions can work with their hands or build a business.

The Vedic sign of Dhanus shows a love of travel and a touch of glamour; your mind is broad and you love to teach and to learn. Your Vedic mansions are Shatabhishak, which denotes intuition and psychic ability, and Purva Bhadra, which means you are headstrong and able to cope with hardship. You are a lover of books and poetry.

The Native American Snow Goose of the Turtle clan indicates a traditional outlook and a regal air, and that you are a hard worker with a love of family life. This changes to the inventive, eccentric Otter on the last day of Capricorn. The West African sign of the Harvest and the Granary makes you careful to store up what you need for a rainy day. This combination indicates belief in yourself and self-reliance.

The Celtic Fir suggests a strong-minded but vulnerable personality, and the Apple indicates a stylish, refined, and sensual nature that is also self-reliant. Elm Capricorns are a little distant with new people. The Norse runic sign of Eihwaz makes you a stickler for detail but also farsighted and protective.

JANUARY ~ AQUARIUS
FROM THE 20TH ONWARD

The air sign of Aquarius makes you independent and self-reliant, with a keen intellect and an interest in a wide range of topics. The Chinese Ox sign adds much-needed practicality and a hardworking element, while the receptive earth element gives you a keen eye for what looks good and the ability to find ingenious answers to difficult problems.

The adventurous Vedic sign of Dhanus rules the first day of your sign, but the rest belongs to Makara, which gives you a practical and hardworking streak, plus more ambition and desire for success than outsiders might suspect. Purva Bhadra mansion makes you a lover of literature and poetry, but also headstrong and sometimes unrealistic. Your karma leads to some areas of suffering in your life. The mansion of Uttara Bhadra gives you an excellent mind and good speaking abilities in addition to courage, fighting spirit, and the ability to shoulder responsibilities.

The Native American Otter of the Butterfly clan makes you clever, bold, playful, and helpful, and gives you a delightful sense of humor and a clear and logical mind. The Baobab Tree of West Africa endows you with authority, honesty, humanity, and a realistic attitude.

The Celtic Elm can make you a little distant and detached; the Cypress ensures that you are independent, a little special, and rather attractive to look at, but with a somewhat haughty demeanor. You need others to be as straightforward as you are. The Norse runic sign of Pertho makes it hard for you to understand yourself at times—and occasionally you will be a complete mystery to others. Aquarians born under Algiz are even more dreamy! However, you can put your mind, hands, and skills to solve almost anything when the need arises.

JULY

JULY ~ CANCER
FROM THE 1ST TO THE 22ND

No man or woman is an island, and that is especially true for those born under the water sign of Cancer—you need to have your loved ones around you. Your shrewd common sense and caution make you an excellent businessperson. The Chinese sign of the Sheep makes you intuitive, creative, and hardworking, and the receptive earth element can bring success and leadership in business or the arts.

The Vedic sign of Mithuna gives you excellent communication ability and a touch of magic when dealing with the public, but it can also make you slightly fickle. The Vedic mansion of Magha makes your personality stronger and more outgoing than it

otherwise might be; the sexy Purva Phagune mansion can lead to self-indulgence.

The Native American Woodpecker of the Frog clan can make you a little too dependent on your partner and desperate for financial and emotional security. This changes to the glamorous Salmon of the Thunderbird clan before long. Fate can throw those born under the West African sign of the Ancestor into positions of leadership; when the sign changes to the Judge, the likelihood of finding yourself in leadership positions is increased, as is your willpower.

Your Celtic tree signs start with the Apple, which adds grace and style but can make you worry about small matters. This changes to the Fir, which indicates a stronger, more ambitious personality, but the vulnerability is still there under the surface. The final Celtic tree sign is the Elm, which indicates a certain naive candor. The Norse runic sign of Fehu brings prosperity and luck, allied to a generous nature; those under the sign of Uruz have a passionate and somewhat wild side to their nature.

JULY ~ LEO

FROM THE 23RD ONWARD

The cheerful, outgoing fire sign of Leo is in evidence at this time, giving you ambition and a longing for the good things of life, but also generosity, kindness, and a glorious sense of humor. Your

greatest love is reserved for your children. The Chinese sign of the receptive Earth Sheep gives you an artistic eye and the ability to work very hard indeed. The earth element makes for efficiency, a scientific turn of mind, and a love of animals.

The Vedic sign of Mithuna endows you with excellent communication skills and a flirtatious manner. This sign eventually changes to Karkarta, which suggests the classic homemaker and family person. The first mansion for your sign is Purva Phagune, which indicates sexuality and a touch of self-indulgence; this changes to Uttara Phalguni, which signifies a quick mind and a generous nature but sometimes a bad choice of friends.

The Native American Salmon of the Thunderbird clan gives you the ability to get to the heart of any matter. You make powerful friends, but also powerful enemies, despite your well-meaning and generous nature. The West African

sign of the Judge denotes decisiveness, enthusiasm, and energy, but it can lead to boastfulness if you are not careful.

The first Celtic tree sign in the sequence is the stately Elm, which can make you appear abrupt and brusque when all you are doing is protecting your own tender feelings. This soon changes to the Cypress, which puts you where the action is. A show-business career would be indicated for some. The Norse runic sign of Uruz means that you are constantly involved in outrageous adventures. This changes on the last day to the powerful sign of Thurisaz.

JUNE

JUNE ~ GEMINI
FROM THE 1ST TO THE 21ST

The air sign of Gemini suggests that you are an excellent communicator who is capable of doing many things at the same time, but who may suffer in relationship matters. The Chinese Horse makes you an excellent salesperson, with a love of travel and a need for freedom. This is enhanced by the active fire nature,

which can lead you into a career in the military or a life of travel, change, and adventure.

The Vedic sign of Vrishaba exerts a steadying influence that helps you stick to jobs and relationships when the going gets tough. This gives you the ability to work with your hands as well as with your intellect. The Vedic mansion of Pushya suggests that there is a caring and loving side to your nature, which can lead you into a caring profession. This changes to Ashlesha, which is excellent for those who wish to study astrology or related subjects.

The Native American Deer of the Butterfly clan makes you a tonic to those around you, as you can never be boring; this changes to the home-loving Woodpecker of the Frog clan on the last day. The West African sign of the Market makes you switch between optimism and pessimism, success and sudden losses. This changes to the Ancestor, which makes you overly idealistic but able to advise others.

The first Celtic tree sign is the Ash, which reveals a many-sided personality and a tendency to rush into difficult relationships. This then changes to the Hornbeam, which endows you with charm, eloquence, and a sense of responsibility. The Norse runic sign of Othila suggests that you gain from inheritance, shrewd investments, or business success. The Norse sign of Dagaz, which follows, denotes honesty and success through achievements, plus luck with money.

JUNE ~ CANCER
FROM THE 22ND ONWARD

As a watery Cancerian, you love a full home life with the members of your family around or popping in and out. You are also a shrewd and cautious businessperson. When not working, you love to take your family traveling. The Chinese Horse sign is also a great traveler; the active fire element adds a need for adventure, which, if unfulfilled, can make you moody or hot-tempered.

The Vedic sign of Vrishaba gives you an artistic streak and a talent for cooking and gardening, in addition to a need for a stable life. This soon changes to the chatty and outgoing sign of Mithuna, which adds versatility and restlessness. The Vedic mansion of Ashlesha attracts some of you to astrology and similar subjects, and it can make you an idealist. The mansion of Magha signifies artistic talent with a touch of arrogance.

The Native American Woodpecker of the Frog clan makes you an affectionate parent who finds it hard to let the little ones go when they grow up. Woodpeckers enjoy listening to music. The West African sign of the Ancestor can lead to depression when life doesn't live up to your expectations—you may need to work at maintaining a realistic attitude.

The Celtic tree sign of the Fig ensures that you want to be the center of a large and happy family, but this soon changes to the Birch, which brings artistic talent and also common sense. The final Celtic tree is the Apple, which makes you fear change and unpredictable events.

The lucky Norse runic sign of Dagaz also adds to your idealism, giving you intuition and a desire for spiritual advancement; Fehu, the sign that follows, brings prosperity.

L

LEO

JULY 23 TO AUGUST 23
SYMBOL: THE LION
RULING PLANET: THE SUN
GROUPS: POSITIVE, FIRE, FIXED

Your nature is generous, outgoing, humorous, and creative, but your standards can be high, which can make you seem arrogant or dismissive of others. You are a charismatic leader with great ability to make things happen.

You are an excellent organizer and an energetic entrepreneur. You have a talent for seeing the big picture and are usually able to attract people to your projects—there is always someone there to carry out the details of your plan. At work you are energetic and efficient, but you can become irritated when things don't go your way. Famous Leos include Napoleon Bonaparte and Henry Ford.

You are a good friend and are very keen to share your experiences and advice with others. You like to be the leader in your social circle and you are not adverse to climbing social and corporate ladders. Leos' love of things larger than life may mean that they sometimes exaggerate their talents and skills.

The challenge for Leos is to realize that they already have many powerful gifts, and that those gifts do not really need to be advertised—they should simply be allowed to grow at a comfortable pace. Leos who do not understand this may sometimes

---

ASTROLOGICAL COMPATIBILITY

WHAT SUN SIGN ARE YOU? Leo

WHO ARE YOUR FRIENDS? Gemini, Libra

WHO ARE YOUR LOVERS? Aries, Sagittarius

---

feel anxious about whether or not they can live up to their own publicity!

You are also highly creative, seeking to create on a large scale. Jobs that attract you are often in sales, promotion, and publicity. Your love of theater and the production of drama can also lead you toward the world stage, as it did for Leo entrepreneur Samuel Goldwyn. With your dynamic and expansive energy, you are also attracted to an acting or singing career. Mae West and Robert Redford are two famous Leos.

Leos need an audience and constant adulation. When they feel that they are not receiving enough praise and attention, Leos become very unhappy and edgy. A challenge for Leos is to realize that they do not need this attention to feel complete and secure. They may need to learn to shift their attention away from themselves and to focus on those closest to them.

You enjoy your family life and are deeply attached to your children. You tend to get bored with the details of family life, though, and will be more than willing to delegate tedious chores. In love, you are passionate, but you may have a habit of falling for the wrong type of person until you learn better; when you find the right person, you are steadfast and faithful.

Being an expansive personality, you may be the last of the big spenders, but you always earn enough to make up the shortfall. You have a great love of quality and beauty, and you have no problems sharing your possessions with your friends and family.

As the Lion is Leos' astrological symbol, they are usually physically attractive. One of their crowning glories may well be a full head of hair that frames their face, enhancing their charm and beauty.

LIBRA

SEPTEMBER 23 TO OCTOBER 23
SYMBOL: THE SCALES
RULING PLANET: VENUS
GROUPS: POSITIVE, AIR, CARDINAL

Being ruled by the Scales, it is no wonder that you often see every side of an argument and find it difficult to make up your mind. A particular challenge for Librans is choosing the right path for themselves, as it is very important for them to make the right decision.

Your charm and ability to handle people make you an excellent agent or arbitrator. At your most balanced, you have a great talent for diplomacy. Great Librans include Mahatma Gandhi and Eleanor Roosevelt.

You have great tact and tend to have rewarding, long-term friendships. You love both hosting social gatherings and being completely alone. Balance is the key feature of your personality, so when you are feeling unhappy or dissatisfied, try to rebalance your life. For example, if the social whirl is becoming too much to handle, take time to be by yourself and enjoy some solitude for a while.

However, Librans tend not to like being alone too much, so they sometimes grab at unsuitable friendships and relationships simply to avoid being on their own. Librans are very sensitive socially—this is why they have such a great ability to understand people. Their advice is often well worth listening to. However, the flip side is that they can get easily offended and become distant and judgmental.

When you feel unbalanced you may find that you start thinking too much about your problems—they seem to revolve around in your head without resolution. This may make you appear aloof.

ASTROLOGICAL COMPATIBILITY

WHAT SUN SIGN ARE YOU? Libra
WHO ARE YOUR FRIENDS? Leo, Sagittarius
WHO ARE YOUR LOVERS? Gemini, Aquarius

Start making decisions about what you really want in your life—this will help you feel that you are no longer rudderless and unfocused.

At work, you are happiest when among those who encourage you to make the most of your considerable talents. You are a great team player and an asset to any organization. However, to keep your interest engaged, seek to continually develop your job skills. A Libran challenge is to avoid procrastination. Make timetables for yourself and learn to keep to them! Remember to make decisions for yourself—do not give anyone else the power to make the decisions in your life that you should be making.

At home, you are best with a protective and loving partner, but you can also enjoy your own company. You are excellent at keeping the peace in your family circle and being diplomatic in family crises. Your challenge is to avoid manipulating those closest to you—it is better to gently encourage them to adopt a particular viewpoint or path and then step away. You have a strong desire to please others and a strong desire to protect those less fortunate than you.

Your excellent taste means that your appearance and your home are always in fashion.

You can spend money freely, but you are quite lucky with finances, so you can usually find a way out of trouble.

M

MARCH

MARCH ~ PISCES

FROM THE 1ST TO THE 20TH

The water sign of Pisces indicates that your values are more spiritual than material. You are both artistic and creative, and you can live a somewhat chaotic lifestyle. The Chinese sign of the receptive Wood Rabbit implies obstinacy and more of a temper than a February Piscean has, but it also makes you refined and tasteful, and gives you a talent for counseling others.

The Vedic sign of Kumbha is in operation at this time, and this gives you an original and inventive turn of mind plus a friendly and humanitarian nature. The Vedic mansion of Ashwini rules the start of this period, endowing you with a somewhat adventurous spirit and a tendency to be outspoken. This soon changes to the Bharani mansion, which gives you artistic talent—this can lead to honor, but you must beware of losses.

The Native American Cougar of the Frog clan ensures that you are entirely comfortable with the spiritual world, but it can make it difficult for you to express your feelings, including your affection to those you love. The West African sign of the Wealth of Amber and Silver gives you an inventive mind and a need for freedom; this changes to the Family, which warms your personality and encourages you to look after your community.

The Celtic Willow tree sign indicates a strong sixth sense and an interest in dreams, spells, and mysteries. This changes to the Lime tree, which also suggests spirituality and mystery, but which makes you something of a perfectionist. The Norse runic sign of Tiwaz gives you strength and the ability to keep promises. Berkana, the sign following, is especially associated with motherhood and a happy home life.

MARCH ~ ARIES
FROM THE 21ST ONWARD

The active, energetic fire sign of Aries suggests that you can rush in headfirst where angels fear to tread. You are honest, humorous, and kind, but you can be so focused on your goals that you walk over others while achieving them. The Chinese sign is the Rabbit, which gives you a touch of class and a need for close personal relationships; the receptive wood element can involve you in causes.

The original, eccentric, and slightly obstinate nature of the Vedic sign of Kumba is in residence at the start of your sign, but it soon gives way to the gentle sign of Meena, which brings a mystical and spiritual element into your nature. The first of your Vedic mansions is Bharani, which indicates talent, but also suggests that arguments and lawsuits may plague you. This is quickly followed by Krittika, which brings success, respect, and fame, but can put you in the line of fire where politics is concerned.

The Native American Red Hawk of the Thunderbird clan gives you energy and makes you a dangerous person to have a falling out with. Your farsightedness enables you to make a success of an idea. The West African sign of the Family adds idealism and a need to look after the wider community by teaching and leading.

One Celtic tree, Oak, rules only the first day of your sign. It gives generosity, practicality, and a touch of intuition. After this, the Hazel takes over. It indicates an enthusiastic, charismatic nature, but also flightiness in love. The Norse runic sign of Berkana, which makes family life and the need for a happy home paramount, starts this period; this changes to Ehwaz, which signifies a person whose purposes are high, but who has a wild streak under the surface.

MAY

MAY ~ TAURUS
FROM THE 1ST TO THE 21ST

The practical earth sign of Taurus shows that you are creative, a lover of beautiful things, a family person, and a reliable worker, but you would be the first to agree about your stubborn determination. Your Chinese Snake sign denotes a reserved and private nature, with the inventive mind that is typical of the backroom worker. However, the fire element adds extroversion, enterprise, and energy—in the receptive mode, this can make you a talented performer with a great voice.

Your Vedic sign is Mesha, which adds impulsiveness, courage, kindness, and a sense of humor, but also a slightly self-centered attitude. The mansion of Ardra brings honor and wealth through marriage, but a career with many ups and downs. Punarvasu gives you a spirited, courageous nature and keen intelligence. Sudden fame is possible, but so is a sudden loss of fortune.

The Native American Beaver of the Turtle clan rules most of this period, ensuring that you take partnerships and family relationships very seriously. The West African sign of Small Services to the Neighborhood denotes the ability to be a leader in your community; later, this changes to the sign of the Market, which signifies a need for financial and emotional security due to a fluctuating pattern of work.

The first Celtic tree is the Poplar, which indicates that you learn and grow by experience. This changes to the Sweet Chestnut, which

says that you are organized and capable, but apt to change your mind unexpectedly or do two things at once. The Norse runic sign is gentle Laguz, which is imaginative, emotional, and understanding; later, this changes to Inguz, which indicates that tradition, family life, and your home will always mean a lot to you.

MAY ~ GEMINI

FROM THE 22ND ONWARD

The air sign of Gemini makes you gregarious, chatty, versatile, and intelligent, but apt to make bad choices in relationships because you tend to hope that your lovers are nicer than they actually are. The Chinese Snake sign ensures that you keep important secrets to yourself while appearing outgoing and friendly. The receptive fire element gives you a touch of glamour and a love of show business, plus talent and a desire to be among exciting and talented people.

The Vedic sign of Mesha gives those at the start of the period an impulsive and adventurous nature. The Vrishaba group, later in the period, is more settled and less apt to make changes just for the sake of it. The mansion of Parnavasu ensures that you have a lively nature and keen intelligence, and it makes fame a distinct possibility. The mansion of Pushya denotes a caring and loving nature.

The Native American Deer of the Butterfly clan makes you an excellent friend who can counsel others without judging them, but you can jump from one idea to another at the drop of a hat. The West African Market sign advises you not to get into relationships that don't offer you a future.

The Celtic tree sign of the Sweet Chestnut shows that you are very capable, but that you can switch paths rapidly and unexpectedly; the Mountain Ash means that you have many sides to your nature—you may live a double life. The Norse runic sign of Inguz makes family life, tradition, and history important to you; for those born under the sign of Othila, property, inheritance, trade, and commerce become important and valuable.

MEDICINE WHEEL

Animal totem astrology is an active system, one that encourages zealous exploration of the world of humans and the world of nature. Native Americans have always been encouraged to experience life from all perspectives—to embrace each of the animal totems at some point in their lives. This means consciously taking on another animal totem's perspective of life in order to learn to appreciate its unique gifts and powers. You can use the system yourself for self-development.

Specific animal totems can be selected if you require specific powers or healing medicine. People who have experienced and

embraced the unique powers of all twelve birth totems will have learned all that is required on the conscious plane, and will be ready to be transported to a higher spiritual plane in their next life.

If you choose to experience life from a particular animal totem's perspective for a while, you will gain some of the power of that animal totem. If, for example, you are enduring difficult times—ill health, stress, or a negative emotional state—you can focus on a person with an animal totem different from your own. As you focus and try to adopt the other person's life perspective, you will start to gain some of the other totem's power.

Once you have acquired an animal totem's power, you will have access to that totem's medicine. The text below tells you which animal totem to choose when you are in need of healing medicine. For example, if you feel that you are too passive and need to take some action in your life, try to see from the perspective of a Beaver. Gather about you symbols of the Beaver, spend time with someone who has this animal totem, find out what its affinities in the plant and animal kingdoms are, and keep them nearby.

Hawk for LOGICAL PERSPECTIVE • *Power:* The ability to heighten your awareness, your vision, and your perception of your environment. *Medicine:* Use when a logical or objective perspective is required rather than an emotional response.

Beaver for HARD WORK • *Power:* The ability to appreciate material achievement through planned and methodical work. *Medicine:* Use when action or hard work is called for.

Deer for UNCONDITIONAL LOVE • *Power:* The ability to be gentle and gracious, and to influence others and endear yourself to them. *Medicine:* Use when unconditional love and acceptance are required.

Woodpecker for INTUITION • *Power:* The ability to stay in balance and true to yourself regardless of the situation. *Medicine:* Use when intuition or a strong inner voice is required.

Salmon for COURAGE • *Power:* The ability to experience fully your primal and vital energies. *Medicine:* Use when courage, strength, and leadership are called for, and/or to balance sexual urges.

Brown Bear for TENACITY • *Power:* The ability to draw on your physical and emotional strength when required. *Medicine:* Use when hard work, tenacity, and trustworthiness are required. Use in times of adversity.

Raven for TRANSFORMING LIFE • *Power:* The ability to inject magic and renewed faith into your life. *Medicine:* Use when stuck in nonproductive situations, and/or if you want to transform a mundane life.

Snake for EMBRACING CHANGE • *Power:* The ability to adapt easily, transform, and experience change in your life. *Medicine:* Use when experiencing change, to enable you to stop resisting and willingly embrace the new.

Owl for SEEING CLEARLY • *Power:* The ability to see clearly in times of uncertainty, deception, or political unrest. *Medicine:* Use when facing your darkest fears or to see and understand the whole truth of a matter.

Snow Goose for PATIENCE • *Power:* The ability to act when the time is right. *Medicine:* Use when patience is called for, or when you need to adhere to a set of principles while making a decision.

Otter for FUN AND FREEDOM • *Power:* The ability to connect with your inner child and to find joy, passion, and a sense of freedom. *Medicine:* Use when imagination or innovation is required and to put fun back into your everyday life.

Wolf for PROTECTION • *Power:* The ability to follow your instincts and intuition rather than your intellect. *Medicine:* Use when experiencing physical danger, or to protect others from an immediate threat.

MONKEY

THE WITTY, CLEVER MONKEY
1920, 1932, 1944, 1956, 1968, 1980, 1992, 2004, 2016
ENERGY: YANG
ELEMENT: METAL
TIME: 3:00 P.M.–5:00 P.M.
MONTH: AUGUST
DIRECTION: WEST/SOUTHWEST
SEASON: EARLY FALL

Monkeys are renowned for their keen intellects and lively, comic personalities. No challenge is too great for these motivated, ingenious intellectuals. Give a problem to a Monkey and you will be presented with a solution and a plan of action before others have even started thinking about the task.

Monkeys detest routine and get bored easily with the status quo. They like to test the boundaries in every possible situation. Monkeys like change; they take risks and can live their lives quite differently from most other people. Their principle is to break the rules, live for the moment, and, above all, have fun. Monkeys rarely show their serious side; if they do, they are probably either acting or joking. Their excitement, optimism, and daredevil approach to life are irrepressible, and they make a strong impression on everyone they meet. Monkeys may also have a keen wit and be skilled at comedy.

The Monkey ascendant for those born between 3:00 P.M. and 5:00 P.M.

Having the Monkey as your ascendant sign will add mental agility to your personality.

Monkeys at their best Confident, funny, inventive, clever, vibrant, motivating, sociable, sexual, versatile

Monkeys at their worst Risky, restless, manipulative, immature, deceitful, mischievous, unpredictable, fickle

Monkey's ninth position at Buddha's side denotes mental agility. Monkeys have quick, lively intellects and sharp wits that few can match. They spend their days scheming and hatching outrageous plots and ingenious plans; they are not above manipulating others to get their way. Monkeys like to defy convention and lead life to the beat of their own drum.

Character traits of Monkeys Intelligent, witty, entertaining, inquisitive, energetic, optimistic, sexual, competitive, lively, inventive, sociable, risk-taking, talkative, enthusiastic, generous, versatile, restless

Life challenge for Monkeys To develop self-discipline for their project and self-control in their relationships.

The Monkey lover Monkeys are charmers and naughty lovers, and they like to lead promiscuous lifestyles. As they may lack morals, anything usually goes in their love life. They often attract the unusual in sexual pleasures, and the mysterious in lovers. Variety and quantity are the keys to a happy love life for Monkeys. As Monkeys are quite competitive, they will thrill to the challenge of new conquests, but will run a mile at the first sign of physical struggle with other suitors.

The Monkey family member It is rare to see a domesticated Monkey, and even rarer to see a happily domesticated Monkey. Should Monkeys choose to settle down, it will only be to secure a home base from which to venture forth in search of fun and adventure. As they hate convention and routine, they will put a lot of energy into keeping their home life exciting. Expect an open-house environment where many people from all walks of life are invited home—indefinitely. Children will identify with the eternal child within their Monkey parent.

The Monkey friend Sociable and entertaining, Monkeys demonstrate the extreme in extroversion. They hate their own company and will, therefore, collect lots of friends and keep in constant contact with them. With their witty and lively conversations, Monkeys are never boring to be around. It is rare to find someone who feels ambivalent about Monkeys. You can be sure they will keep their friends happily entertained with all their clever antics.

The Monkey at work Monkeys usually win and lose fortunes repeatedly throughout their lives, as they are attracted to the riskiest of schemes. In the workplace, Monkeys hate routine and hard work and have short attention spans. They are not the easiest or the most pleasant to work with, but are sure to add brightness to any dull office environment. At their best, Monkeys are exceptional planners and organizers who need lots of variety and challenge to keep their highly active minds engaged and motivated.

Ideal occupations for Monkeys Comedian, entertainer, actor, traveler, photographer, social columnist, journalist

The five Monkey types

WOOD MONKEYS • 1944, 2004 • The stability of wood dilutes some of Monkeys' rather eccentric and rash traits. Wood Monkeys are more focused, less erratic, and hence more capable than the average Monkey. They are the most comfortable and secure Monkeys to be around.

FIRE MONKEYS • 1956, 2016 • Monkeys' natural metal element combines with fire to form quite powerful and ruthless individuals. Fire Monkeys are passionate and don't mind applying a little physical force as a last resort. Fire Monkeys are the most competitive and dangerous of the Monkeys.

EARTH MONKEYS • 1968 • The effect of the earth element is to make these Monkeys fairly interested in pursuing their intellectual development. Earth Monkeys read widely and are likely to hold numerous academic qualifications from an early age. They are diligent and focused.

METAL MONKEYS • 1920, 1980 • The effect of double metal is to make these Monkeys quite ambitious, intelligent, and very good with money. Metal Monkeys are extremely confident of their own abilities and have little trouble convincing others of their talents.

WATER MONKEYS • 1932, 1992 • The water element ensures that these Monkeys are more considerate and more understanding of their effect and, therefore, less inclined to ridicule anyone. Water Monkeys are team players, able to cooperate and to keep a check on their emotions.

Famous Monkeys

MEL GIBSON, ACTOR/DIRECTOR

Mel Gibson, a Fire Monkey, embodies the fun-loving joker in all Monkeys. He is renowned on movie sets for playing endless pranks and tricks on his costars. He is also quite competitive and enjoys physical challenges, which is evident in many of his movie roles.

BETTE DAVIS, ACTOR

Bette Davis is a legend among film stars. As a typical Earth Monkey, she exhibited a more serious side to her personality, and her mental agility was evident in the roles she played on-screen. Like many Monkeys, she had a strong effect—the public either loved her or loathed her.

RELATIONSHIP CHART FOR MONKEYS

Monkey + Rating		Potential for harmony in love, friendship, and professional life
Rat	Best friend	Each will admire the other's quick wit and superior intelligence. Provided Rat remains tolerant of Monkey's antics, these two will be able to initiate many schemes and ingenious plans together.
Dragon	Best friend	Dragon will be attracted to Monkey's charm and wit, and Monkey to Dragon's personal power. Monkey will be happy for Dragon to dominate, and the two will live easily together.
Ox	Good but needs work	Ox will be fascinated by Monkey's sparkling wit, and Monkey will appreciate the attention. However, the attraction will be only brief, as Monkey craves change and Ox respects routine.
Rabbit	Challenging	Both are witty and inventive, which will ensure an attraction. However, Monkey will always be breaking social rules and norms, and Rabbit won't tolerate this for long.
Snake	Positive	There is enough mental dexterity to ensure the success of these two as business partners. Snake will provide the logic and Monkey the calculated risks.
Horse	Good but needs work	Each will be attracted to the other's energy and enthusiasm. However, Horses wear their hearts on their sleeves and can be a little gullible, which the secretive Monkey will not appreciate.
Sheep	Positive	Monkeys will soon have Sheep laughing at themselves and more willing to take risks, while Sheep will instill some morals in Monkeys and curb their excesses.
Monkey	Good but needs work	These two deserve each other and will feel they have found their match in wit and intelligence. As long as they can resist feeding the rivalry between them, a relationship will develop.
Rooster	Positive	There is a lot of potential with this pairing, as both are vibrant entertainers. Roosters and Monkeys need to restrain themselves from judging each other too quickly to ensure that they see all the qualities the other offers.
Dog	Challenging	Dog will be attracted to Monkey's intelligence, but will soon find Monkey devious and insincere. Monkey will be attracted to Dog's eagerness to please, but will find Dog's morals hard to abide.
Pig	Challenging	There will be a lot of attraction between these two. However, Monkeys will not be able to resist using easygoing Pigs as the butt of their jokes. Pigs will soon be left feeling hurt and dejected.
Tiger	Archenemy	Both are competitive and impatient daredevils, which guarantees many calamities. Tiger will be supersensitive to Monkey's pranks, and Monkey will soon get bored with Tiger's lack of wisdom.

N

NOVEMBER

NOVEMBER ~ SCORPIO
FROM THE 1ST TO THE 22ND

The water sign of Scorpio knows no middle way, so your loves and hates are equally intense, and your opinions are strong. The Chinese

sign for this month is the Pig, which makes you look mild—it actually hides an acute mind. The receptive water aspect ensures that your head for business is allied to a love of the arts. You are happier working behind the scenes than out in front.

Your Vedic sign is Thula, which enhances your love of art and music; it can also make you a little indecisive at times. The first mansion is Jyestha, which endows you with intelligence and potential success in a military or political career. This soon changes to Mula, which denotes a keen mind and good judgment, then to Purvashada, which represents leadership and an interest in justice.

Your Native American sign is the Serpent of the Frog clan, which means you have a talent for teaching, along with the ability to transform your life when the need arises. The sign changes to the Elk of the Thunderbird clan, which gives you a regal air, a great deal of insight, and teaching ability. Your West African sign will be either the Distance, which shows that your passions and instincts are strong, or the Child of the World, which signifies generosity, enthusiasm, and a touch of arrogance.

Your Celtic tree sign is the Walnut, which offers courage, understanding, and a love of home and family. This changes to the Yew, which indicates a reserved outer manner with strong passions raging beneath. The Chestnut, the next tree sign, represents determination hidden beneath a shy exterior. The Norse runic sign of Hagalaz suggests that your life will not run particularly smoothly. This changes to Nauthiz, which brings luck when it is needed.

NOVEMBER ~ SAGITTARIUS
FROM THE 23RD ONWARD

The fire sign of Sagittarius denotes an enthusiastic, humorous, and generous personality. Your need for freedom means that you choose a job that takes you out and about—this can delay marriage and parenthood until later in life. Your Chinese sign, the receptive water Pig, makes you deeper and more intellectual than outsiders might realize. It gives you an artistic and musical streak, as well as a sense of timing where business matters are concerned. You may have to learn a different language during the course of your life.

The Vedic sign is Vrishchika, which ensures that you can keep secrets and also keep your innermost feelings hidden when the need arises. The mansion of Uttarashada suggests musical and artistic ability, and it can make you a good dancer. Your leadership qualities can take you to the top, but a touch of laziness may hold you back.

Your Native American sign is the stately Elk of the Thunderbird clan, which makes you quiet when young but more outgoing later. This sign gives you a strong sense of justice. Elk people are outwardly friendly but secretive about their deepest feelings. The West African sign of the Child of the World gives you a cheerful, enthusiastic nature and the ability to attract help and admiration from others.

The Celtic tree sign is the Mountain Ash, which denotes a somewhat double-sided nature, at once reserved and compliant but also intelligent, self-reliant, and rather critical of others. The Norse runic sign is Nauthiz, which suggests that you will have some lessons to learn in this life, but that luck is also often on your side.

O

OCTOBER

OCTOBER ~ LIBRA
FROM THE 1ST TO THE 23RD

Gentle, indecisive Libra is an air sign, which means that you have an active mind allied to an artistic nature. The Chinese sign for this month is the active earth Dog, which gives excellent counseling

abilities, but also a naive and trusting nature, which can make you a prey to less scrupulous types. The earth active element adds creativity allied to practicality, which leads to success.

Your Vedic sign is the modest and hardworking Kanya, which gives you a perfectionist nature that can be a little difficult to live with. The mansion of Anuradha brings a fluctuating income, a helpful nature, and an interest in astrology and related subjects. This changes to Jyestha, which ensures intelligence and potential honors in a political or military career.

Your Native American sign is the Raven of the Butterfly clan, which indicates intuition and a tendency to withdraw when you are hurt. The West African sign of the Traveler can lead to travel or to an interest in spiritual matters. This soon changes to the sign of the Distance, which brings success once you have overcome early anxieties.

The Celtic tree signs start with the Hazel, which adds passion and charisma. This soon changes to the Mountain Ash, which belongs to a strong personality with a talent for secrecy. This is followed by the Maple, which belongs to a forceful, intelligent, and independent person who prefers to live by his own rules. The final tree is the Walnut, signifying courage and magnetism but also a love of home life. The Norse runic sign of

Gebo adds generosity, helpfulness, and a touch of luck. This changes to Wunjo, which also indicates luck, especially in love relationships.

OCTOBER ~ SCORPIO
FROM THE 24TH ONWARD

The water sign of Scorpio is noted for its power. Many military and political leaders come under this sign, but so do wonderful homemakers and employees. The Chinese sign is the active earth Dog, which can make you naive and sentimental, but also extremely helpful and hardworking. Your creative talent means that you can work with your hands as well as with your mind.

The Vedic sign is Kanya, suggesting an eye for detail and a love of books and music—it can also lead to an interest in health and healing. This changes to the artistic sign of Thula, which can make you a little double-sided or indecisive, but clever in business and with an eye for what looks good. The mansion at this time is Jyestha, which denotes intelligence, and honors in a military or political career. Sudden gains and losses are possible throughout your life.

Your Native American sign is the Serpent of the Frog clan, which gives you intelligence, but can also give you an extremely bad temper. You can adapt yourself to most circumstances when you need to. The West African sign is the Distance, which is a strong sign—your natural impulsiveness, allied to sudden changes in

circumstances, ensures that your life will never be boring.

The Celtic tree sign is the charismatic Walnut, suggesting that you are hardworking and efficient, but can be overly critical of others. Your charm and sensual looks attract others, but you are not fickle. The Norse runic sign is Hagalaz, which also suggests that you will have storms to weather during your life; the key to coping with this is to tap into your remarkable capabilities.

OTTER

Native Americans view the otter as one of the most playful and friendly animals in the wild. Otters appear to live their lives in true bliss. Relaxing and sunning themselves one moment, the next moment they are quickly attending to the chores of hunting and eating before moving on to play and cooling themselves in water.

Like their animal totem, Otter people are clever and gentle and have keen intellects, as well as a playful, inquisitive approach to life and a sociable nature. Like their metal and color affinity, silver, Otter people are shiny, flexible, and beautiful to behold. They are viewed as precious additions to a family and community because of their dynamism and their ability to attract good fortune and abundance.

Otters possess strong powers of perception, intuition, and vision. They display true affection for others, with flowing emotional energy that can make them passionate and ardent lovers. Otter people often have psychic abilities, with a knack for accurately predicting the future.

Otter people make good friends and lively companions, particularly during

SEASON	The heart of winter—a time of cleansing, purification, and reflection
SEASON TOTEM	White Buffalo
SEASON ELEMENT	Air
BIRTH TIME	January 20–February 18 Northern Hemisphere July 23–August 22 Southern Hemisphere
BIRTH TIME ELEMENT	Air
ELEMENTAL CLAN	Butterfly
ENERGY FLOW	Active
AFFINITIES	Color: silver/gray Plant: aspen tree Mineral: silver
GIFTS	Imaginativeness, humanitarianism, youthfulness, perceptiveness, curiosity, empathy, passion
CHALLENGES	Sensitivity, idealism, impracticality, intensity
LIFE PATH	To develop your latent psychic powers consciously, maintain an easy flow of emotion, and regularly touch base with the physical world around you.

hard times, as they act as motivators and lift the mood and outlook of everyone around them. Rarely judgmental, Otter people are open-minded, empathic, tolerant, lighthearted, and generous, and they follow the call to humanitarian causes in their choice of career.

Otter people adapt easily to new people and surroundings and prefer to live life at a lively pace. They are independent, individualistic, and true extroverts, which is reflected in their active energy type. They need only rare moments of solitude in order to touch base effectively with their feelings and spirituality.

IDEAL PAIRINGS	
Otter +	Relationship potential
Deer	This pair has the potential for a fun-filled and harmonious life together. There is little capacity for friction in either.
Raven	Both have strong humanitarian values and will find in each other the support and encouragement they require.
Hawk	Both are quite active and optimistic individuals. Their energies will easily match, and each will strengthen the other.
Owl	This pair will make a good match. Owl will provide wisdom and the sensible touch, while Otter will provide Owl with youthful enthusiasm.
Salmon	**Complement.** Each will make a loyal and supportive companion to the other. A natural attraction and kinship exists between these two animal totems.

CHALLENGING PAIRINGS	
Otter +	Relationship potential
Snow Goose	Both have air as their season element, so they have similar lessons to learn in life. They can help each other—provided both are mature enough to respect their differences.
Wolf	Otter will fruitlessly endeavor to raise Wolf from melancholy states, while Wolf will fail to provide the support Otter requires for achieving goals.
Beaver	They live on opposite sides of the stream. Beaver is industrious and prefers to work. Otter is imaginative and prefers to play.
Woodpecker	Both lack drive and ambition, hence neither will be able to help the other in productive endeavors.
Brown Bear	Otters are optimistic daredevils, while Brown Bears are cynical and far too serious. Neither can meet the other's expectations.
Snake	Snake will constantly be jealous of Otter's popularity and will soon seek the limelight with other, less-attractive companions.
Otter	An Otter pairing with another will bring about a mirroring effect, whereby the best and the worst in each other will be magnified.

OWL

The owl is frequently referred to by Native Americans as the "night eagle" or the "night's friend." A large bird of prey with a distinctive cry, it has huge eyes that give it the power to see through the darkest of nights. Native Americans believe the owl can see and know everything. Sighting one in the wild is a sign that you should become more observant of what can't be seen at a physical level, or that it is time for you to face your darkest fears.

Owl people are intelligent, very observant, and sensible. While young Owls are growing up they may be described as "wise beyond their years," and wisdom is a gift they carry throughout their lives. Owl people have an inner strength and an ability to be both soft and strong in their personalities.

Given their eye for detail and their almost clairvoyant ability to read the thoughts and intentions of others, Owls are very difficult to deceive. They can get to the heart of any matter in record time, leaving others still confused about how they did it and frustrated in any plan to put one over the wise, all-knowing Owl.

SEASON	Late fall—a time of long nights and the arrival of the first snows
SEASON TOTEM	Grizzly Bear
SEASON ELEMENT	Earth
BIRTH TIME	November 22–December 21 Northern Hemisphere May 21–June 20 Southern Hemisphere
BIRTH TIME ELEMENT	Fire
ELEMENTAL CLAN	Thunderbird
ENERGY FLOW	Active
AFFINITIES	Color: black Plant: black spruce pine Mineral: obsidian—volcanic glass/granite
GIFTS	Self-reliance, expressiveness, inquisitiveness, wisdom, justice, sense, intelligence, discretion
CHALLENGES	Conventionalism, intolerance, pride, dominance
LIFE PATH	To cultivate and practice tolerance in your everyday dealings with others, especially those less gifted and developed than you.

The only risks Owl people take in life are those they have calculated thoroughly. Hence, they rarely make a poor decision. Regret is an emotion Owls just don't get to experience.

It's not surprising, then, that in modern society, judges or school principals are often Owl people. Owls have strong ethics and principles and a clear sense of fairness and justice. In addition, they like to be in positions of power—ideally those that will allow them to make decisions about right or wrong, guilt or innocence—and to dispense any punishment due.

IDEAL PAIRINGS

Owl +	Relationship potential
Hawk	Both have a strong sense of right and wrong. They will find their values match and will be happy to live according to their principles and ethics.
Salmon	Both have energy to burn and will find the other stimulating company. Salmon can gain wise counsel from Owl, while Owl will find Salmon has an exciting charm.
Otter	This pair will make a good match. Owl will provide wisdom and the sensible touch, while Otter will provide Owl with youthful enthusiasm.
Raven	Sensible Owl will encourage Raven's strong social conscience. Raven will reward Owl with influential networks and contacts.
Deer	**Complement.** A natural attraction and kinship exists between these two animal totems. Each will make the other a loyal and supportive companion.

CHALLENGING PAIRINGS

Owl +	Relationship potential
Snow Goose	Both will want to dominate the relationship, and antagonism will build over time.
Wolf	Owl will be frustrated and intolerant of Wolf's indecisiveness and sensitivity. Wolf will soon feel it better to go it alone.
Beaver	Each will want to dominate the other in this relationship. Beaver will remain inflexible despite Owl's attempts to exert influence, and Owl will be too proud to give Beaver any ground.
Woodpecker	Owl is too self-reliant for Woodpecker, who will not feel any true union between them. Owl will not find Woodpecker stimulating company.
Brown Bear	These two opinionated and strong-willed individuals will clash on meeting. They will end up as adversaries in most situations.
Snake	Owl and Snake are rivals in any context, and a relationship will bring out the worst in both of them—jealousy and deceitfulness in Snake, and pride and intolerance in Owl.
Owl	Owl pairing with another will bring about a mirroring effect, whereby the best and the worst in each other will be magnified.

OX

THE TENACIOUS, PATIENT OX
1913, 1925, 1937, 1949, 1961, 1973, 1985, 1997, 2009
ENERGY: YIN
ELEMENT: EARTH
TIME: 1:00 A.M.–3:00 A.M.
MONTH: JANUARY
DIRECTION: NORTH/NORTHEAST
SEASON: LATE WINTER

Oxen are direct, principled, and dedicated people who like to tread the well-worn paths of tradition and respectability. They are trustworthy and grounded; when they give you their word, they will not let you down. Their core talent is their enormous reserve of physical energy, which they can skillfully harness and manage over long periods of time.

Apart from their physical strength, Oxen are also endowed with a keen appreciation of beauty. They will often give in to their need to indulge their senses.

The Ox ascendant for those born between 1:00 A.M. and 3:00 A.M. The Ox as the ascendant sign adds practicality, determination, and physical energy to the personality, as well as an appreciation of sensual pleasures.

Oxen at their best Responsible, hardy, sensible, dutiful, eloquent, industrious, persevering, diligent

Oxen at their worst Authoritative, stubborn, biased, intolerant, conservative, complacent, depressive, proud

Character traits of the Ox Reliable, patient, purposeful, conscientious, kind, determined, persevering, hardworking, sensuous, painstaking, dependable, stable, skillful, dexterous, confident, authoritative

Life challenge for Oxen To feel more comfortable with their feelings and be more expressive of their emotions.

Oxen are the most physically powerful and sure-footed animals of the Chinese zodiac. No other sign can match them for physical endurance, tenacity, and patience. Oxen are traditionalists at heart, who take life seriously and will persevere through all manner of hardship to fulfill their goals and obligations.

The Ox lover Work comes first and romance a distant second for the Ox. Hence Oxen are not likely to win or break many hearts during their lifetime, nor do they want to. Monogamy is the only game they want to play. Capable of deep and sensual love, Oxen will settle down quickly into one lifelong, faithful relationship. Oxen are renowned for their stamina and have an intense, sensuous side to their nature. Having an Ox lover means being guaranteed a dependable, protective, and kind partner who puts your needs first.

The Ox family member Oxen make very reliable, stable, and responsible children, siblings, and parents. They love their homes and believe that the family is the nucleus of society. They set high expectations for themselves and others, which can transform them into stern disciplinarians if their values are not shared. Oxen make formidable protectors and dependable providers who will work day and night to ensure that the needs of their family are met. It is through their actions—especially hard work—that Oxen express how much they feel for others.

The Ox friend Kindly Oxen are capable of making everyone around them feel comfortable and secure. They love to entertain, particularly where fine food and wine are on offer. They are happy to indulge themselves as a just reward for all their hard work. Oxen prefer small gatherings to large, and intimate conversations to a lot of chatter. Confident in their social skills, Oxen love to recite entertaining sagas of triumphs over hardship and evil. It's marvelous being around an Ox friend who is in a jovial and expansive mood.

The Ox at work Extremely competent and capable individuals, Oxen shine in the work arena and can remain calm under pressure. As employees, Oxen are respected for their trustworthiness and dependability, and the way they ensure that even the most difficult projects are completed on time. As colleagues, Oxen are generous with their time and assistance (just remember the legend of the Ox, who gladly aided the Rat across the river). As employers, Oxen are open, honest, and demanding. Most of an Ox's employees would claim their greatest work challenges, and hence successes, came with a clearly directed Ox as their superior. Oxen don't require accolades and promotions to maintain their enthusiasm. Their own personal sense of achievement is sufficient to motivate them—along with the occasional pay raise.

Ideal occupations for Oxen Judge, police officer, statistician, administrator, ambulance driver, government worker

The five Ox types

WOOD OXEN • 1925, 1985 • Wood brings even more stability to the Ox's calm character. Wood Oxen are extremely dependable and live life by a very clear and specific code of ethics. They set and reach high goals in all areas of their lives and usually attain material wealth.

FIRE OXEN • 1937, 1997 • The fire element can bring both dangerous volatility and vibrant enthusiasm to the Ox's character. Fire Oxen are ready, able, and willing to express their emotions, especially their anger. Inflamed with passionate creativity, Fire Oxen are a powerhouse of achievement and require a constant stream of new projects to keep them happy.

EARTH OXEN • 1949, 2009 • The double earth element gives these Oxen plenty of resourcefulness and wisdom. They are typical Oxen, displaying all the Ox's core traits. Reliable and steadfast, Earth Oxen know what they want out of life and set out early with quiet patience and hard work to achieve their goals.

METAL OXEN • 1961 • Metal has the effect of strengthening the Ox's core character traits. Blessed with vision and logic, Metal Oxen make extremely capable business leaders. Metal Oxen are the most ambitious and materialistic of all Oxen and will pursue their goals with tenacity.

WATER OXEN • 1913, 1973 • Water brings eloquence, intuition, and reflection—traits it usually lacks—to the Ox's character. Water Oxen will be more focused on others than themselves throughout their lives, displaying competence as counselors or social workers. Wise, caring, and logical, Water Oxen are the most altruistic of the Ox group.

Famous Oxen

PAUL NEWMAN, ACTOR/DIRECTOR

Paul Newman is a Wood Ox who exhibits this Ox's intense goal orientation and ethical approach to life. Devoted to his family, Newman has at the same time maintained highly successful acting and business careers.

RELATIONSHIP CHART FOR OXEN

Ox +	Rating	Potential for harmony in love, friendship, and professional life
Rooster	Best friend	Much success could come from this pairing, as flamboyant Rooster will attend to the social aspects of the relationship, while Ox will attend to the detailed planning and physical work.
Snake	Best friend	Much happiness could result from this pairing. The Ox will provide Snake with stability and physical resources so that they can meet common goals. Snake will entice Ox into lighter moods when necessary.
Rat	Positive	A mutually rewarding partnership in any context. Rat's intelligence and ingenuity will complement Ox's physical tenacity. This pair could achieve much together.
Ox	Good but needs work	For the most part this pairing could work, as neither will ask too much from the other. However, life could become extremely dull, as all Oxen are quite serious.
Tiger	Challenging	In the wild, these two would be natural enemies. Both are physically powerful and will want to dominate the relationship. This could lead to conflict and exhaustion on both parts.
Rabbit	Positive	Rabbit will be happy for Ox to dominate and provide. Rabbit's gentle optimism will act as a soothing balm to Ox's grueling pessimism.
Dragon	Challenging	A powerful but thwarted combination. Ox won't be able to stand Dragon's passion for the unconventional. Dragon will quickly become bored and frustrated with Ox's fixation on routine.
Horse	Challenging	A mutual lack of understanding and respect will unfold quickly with this pairing. Horse will crave freedom and excitement and will soon leave the traditional and authoritative Ox.
Monkey	Good but needs work	Ox will be fascinated by Monkey's sparkling wit, and Monkey will appreciate the attention. However, the attraction will be brief; Monkey craves change and Ox respects routine.
Dog	Positive	These two share values such as loyalty and respect. This pairing could work if Ox could lighten up and if Dog could maintain an understanding of Ox's temperament.
Pig	Good but needs work	Both crave a peaceful and quiet home life. However, Pig may be irresponsible with money, which will frustrate Ox. Unless Pig can learn restraint, Ox will soon leave.
Sheep	Archenemy	Ox will have no respect for the excitable and morally deviant Sheep, who will find no excitement in the dull Ox. This pairing is best avoided, as the values and beliefs of the two parties will be directly opposed.

P

PIG

THE CAREFREE, CONTENTED PIG
1923, 1935, 1947, 1959, 1971, 1983, 1995, 2007, 2019
ENERGY: YIN
ELEMENT: WATER
TIME: 9:00 P.M.–11:00 P.M.
MONTH: NOVEMBER
DIRECTION: NORTH/NORTHWEST
SEASON: EARLY WINTER

Pigs are calm and contented. Stress-free and peace-loving, they are the easiest people to get along with. They like to take life as it comes, focusing on the moment and indulging in everything that delights them. They tend not to set too many goals for themselves, and apply effort only if it will reduce their daily chores instead of increasing them. Pigs are calm, friendly, fun to be with, and undemanding. However, they do like an opulent life and would prefer this to be provided by someone else. They know how to enjoy life to the fullest, and happiness is their most constant emotional state.

The Pig ascendant for those born between 9:00 P.M. and 11:00 P.M. Having the Pig as the ascendant sign means a carefree attitude to life and a focus on enjoyment and self-indulgence.

Pigs at their best Enthusiastic, generous, outgoing, merry, positive, sensual, warmhearted

Pigs at their worst Self-indulgent, hot-tempered, excessive, spendthrift, gullible, debauched, naive, materialistic

Character traits of Pigs Sensual, eager, caring, indulgent,

The twelfth and final position at Buddha's side represents completeness and celebration of the cycle's end. Pigs are the most easily contented and happy-go-lucky of all the Chinese zodiac animals. They are true peacemakers and are talented at bringing divergent groups and individuals together in harmony.

pleasure-seeking, fun, lighthearted, optimistic, peaceful, flexible, warmhearted, understanding, generous, happy, shy, modest

Life challenge for Pigs To set specific goals in their lives and maintain the effort to accomplish those goals.

The Pig lover Pigs are happy to wallow in sensuous lovemaking for long stretches of time and will demonstrate a lot of loving care and deep emotions toward their lovers. As Pigs are also considerate and understanding, they are able to forgive their partners' many trespasses. In return, Pigs look for lovers who are good providers and protectors, and who will be happy to provide Pigs with the means to pursue their sensual indulgences.

The Pig family member "Home sweet home" is where most Pigs really want to be. Pigs are in their element when surrounded by a close and caring family. They are true nurturers, and prefer to stay at home while their partners go off to work. The Chinese believe a Pig brings much happiness to a family and that Pig children are a delight. As parents, Pigs, who are not disciplined themselves, will want their own children to be achievers, and can be a little strict with them to ensure that they learn self-discipline.

The Pig friend As the most affable, easygoing, and undemanding animals of the zodiac, Pigs are assured of many friendships. Their sincerity and concern for others' well-being ensure that they are often sought out for advice, support, and warm company. As a busy social life and indulging in fine food are important to them, Pigs will put much energy into social arrangements. Friends of Pigs can look forward to many picnics, dinner parties, and social gatherings, where fine food will be guaranteed.

The Pig at work If they didn't have to work, Pigs wouldn't. To most Pigs, work is but a means to an end. They rarely put energy into planning their careers, preferring them to unravel unhindered while they keep focused on their family ties and enjoy their friendships. However, Pigs are liked and appreciated by everyone at work and make enthusiastic team members. Always eager to please, particularly where their own work is concerned, Pigs take their individual responsibilities quite seriously. Many Pigs end up pursuing successful careers as independent artists or craftspeople.

Ideal occupations for Pigs Homemaker, child-care worker, nurse, counselor, chef, artist, diplomat, government worker

The five Pig types

WOOD PIGS • 1935, 1995 • The wood element provides an emphasis on Pig's communication skills. Wood Pigs are good at communicating their thoughts and feelings and are able to express their needs. Wood Pigs are encouraged to consider careers as counselors or diplomats in order to use these skills to the fullest.

FIRE PIGS • 1947, 2007 • The fire element gets Pigs moving and adds some bravado and risk taking to their home-loving characters. Fire Pigs are more ambitious than other Pigs and are more likely to seek careers that ensure some travel and moderate adventure. Fire can also heighten Pigs' eagerness, which could lead them into situations they cannot handle.

EARTH PIGS • 1959, 2019 • Earth Pigs are the true homebodies of the Pig family. The big, wide world is of little interest, as they are quite happy to settle down early in life and lead a routine, secure existence. It's the simple, everyday pleasures that Earth Pigs seek.

METAL PIGS • 1971 • Metal provides Pigs with much-needed strength of character and tenacity. Metal Pigs are ambitious, but also fairly sociable. They blend the various areas of their life together well. Metal Pigs have a tendency to be extra stubborn.

WATER PIGS • 1923, 1983 • The double water element heightens Pigs' heavy emotional and intuitive state, making Water Pigs supersensitive and emotionally indulgent. Lost in a world of introspection and prone to depression, Water Pigs may lack the physical and mental fortitude required for lifting themselves out of a rut.

Famous Pigs

DUDLEY MOORE, COMEDIAN/ACTOR/MUSICIAN
Dudley Moore was the model happy-go-lucky, pleasure-seeking Pig, with the wood element enhancing his artistic traits. Like many Pigs, he could be easily swayed and won over by less scrupulous types. His personal life was marked by a number of divorces.

LUCILLE BALL, COMEDIAN/ACTOR
Lucille Ball indulged her humorous Pig personality and chose acting as her career. As a Metal Pig, Lucille Ball displayed more perseverance and tenacity than other Pigs. This was evident in the roles she played: She was able to avoid falling prey to others' schemes.

RELATIONSHIP CHART FOR PIGS

Pig +	Rating	Potential for harmony in love, friendship, and professional life
Rabbit	Best friend	Both have peaceful and tolerant natures and will be able to provide each other with gentle, loving care. Pig will provide strength and openness, and Rabbit practicality.
Sheep	Best friend	Both are sensitive and understanding and will be supportive of each other. The environment will be so tranquil that their creative talents will flourish.
Rat	Good but needs work	Sensuous Pig will revel in Rat's material acquisitions. Rat will enjoy the provider role at first and will then be likely to take Pig for granted, leaving little hope for long-term success.
Ox	Good but needs work	Both crave a peaceful and quiet home life. However, Pig may be irresponsible with money, which will frustrate Ox. Unless Pig can learn restraint, Ox will soon leave.
Tiger	Positive	Home-loving Pig will be happy and appreciative if Tiger acts as provider and protector. Tiger will bask in Pig's esteem and indulgent nature.
Dragon	Positive	This pairing is an example of opposites attracting. Dramatic Dragons will sweep easygoing Pigs off their feet. Pig will reward Dragon with adoration and esteem.
Horse	Positive	This couple will be popular and will have an active social life together. At some point Horse will want to travel abroad and Pig will want to stay at home.
Monkey	Challenging	There will be a lot of attraction between these two. However, Monkeys will not be able to resist using the easygoing Pigs as the butt of their jokes. Pig will soon be left feeling hurt and dejected.
Rooster	Challenging	Pig will be happy for Rooster to rule and will be understanding of Rooster's secret insecurities. Rooster will appreciate Pig's support and will reward Pig generously.
Dog	Positive	Pig will be able to lift the worries from Dog's shoulders, and Dog will be cherished as a faithful protector. There is opportunity for success, if both can avoid moralizing.
Pig	Good but needs work	Two Pigs together will be very happy, but will have little self-control. Each will encourage the other to overindulge in life's pleasures, with little regard for practicalities or consequences.
Snake	Archenemy	Pigs are open and generous with their affection. Snakes are secretive and keep their feelings to themselves. The two just will not be able understand or respect each other.

PISCES

FEBRUARY 19 TO MARCH 20
SYMBOL: THE FISH
RULING PLANET: NEPTUNE
GROUPS: NEGATIVE, WATER, MUTABLE

You may have two sides to your personality, one side being kind, caring, and apt to sacrifice yourself for others. The other side can be surprisingly bossy, but your sensitive nature means that you feel any hurt very deeply and you are quick to understand the feelings of others.

Your challenge is to keep connected to the world and to your friends around you. Pisceans often tend to float away when they do not feel loved or appreciated. As they feel hurt easily, periods of trauma or anxiety may lead them to withdraw from life and avoid their responsibilities. Surprisingly, for such a talented star sign, Pisceans suffer greatly from a low sense of self-esteem, finding it difficult to believe that they are any good at anything.

Pisceans are particularly intuitive and often psychic, with an inner feeling of certainty that there is more out there than meets the eye. This leads them into a deep interest—and occasionally a career in—spiritual subjects.

Many Pisceans, at one point in their life, toy with the idea of being a priest, nun, or other type of spiritual leader. Edgar Cayce and Rudolf Steiner are two such famous Pisceans. As Pisceans' values are spiritual rather than materialistic, they may never make much money.

Other jobs that attract Pisceans include professions where they are not in the limelight, such as nursing, or the exact opposite career choice, such as acting. Famous Piscean actors include Rex Harrison and Sidney Poitier. You also tend to have a poetic or

---

ASTROLOGICAL COMPATIBILITY

WHAT SUN SIGN ARE YOU? Pisces

WHO ARE YOUR FRIENDS? Taurus, Capricorn

WHO ARE YOUR LOVERS? Cancer, Scorpio

musically creative streak. Piscean musicians include classical composers Handel, Chopin, and Rimsky-Korsakov.

Overall, you like to have a job where you can control your hours of work and where you can experience a great deal of variety. Pisceans need to find their direction in life and are particularly good at getting information from others about the best path to tread. They are generally good team players, when given encouragement and space to do their work. They prefer to work alone or in a select group rather than be the leader.

Your partner must understand your need to pursue your interests and your need to leave the house for days at a time when work calls. You seek romantic love, and your intuition becomes a valuable asset in making a relationship that you have committed to work. Your challenge is to develop a sense of practicality, taking control of your career choices and financial decisions, rather than being led.

R

RABBIT

THE FLEXIBLE, BALANCED RABBIT
1915, 1927, 1939, 1951, 1963, 1975, 1987, 1999, 2011
ENERGY: YIN
ELEMENT: WOOD
TIME: 5:00 A.M.–7:00 A.M.
MONTH: MARCH
DIRECTION: EAST
SEASON: SPRING

Rabbits are the intuitive diplomats of Chinese astrology. Blessed with natural style and good taste, they devote many of their resources to their attire and household goods. A secure and harmonious environment is vital for the sensitive Rabbit.

Rabbits like to operate in the background; they would rather observe and reflect than be actively engaged. They will tactfully handle any issue that arises, and will effortlessly manage disputes, generally achieving peaceful resolutions. They make able negotiators and have advanced networking skills.

The Rabbit ascendant for those born between 5:00 A.M. and 7:00 A.M.
The Rabbit as the ascendant sign will bring you added flexibility and balance. Rabbit ascendants are peace lovers and tactful when dealing with others.

Rabbits at their best Discreet, peaceful, perceptive, contemplative, refined, diplomatic, stylish, temperate

Rabbits at their worst Indecisive, snobbish, self-indulgent, secretive, self-focused, condescending, moody, detached, conservative

As the fourth animal to reach Buddha's side, the Rabbit holds the position of harmony and flexibility. Rabbits are generally kind and sensitive characters who detest open conflict, preferring to manage their disputes with diplomacy, intelligence, and tact.

Character traits of Rabbits Diplomatic, peaceful, sensitive, intuitive, reflective, refined, stylish, moderate, caring, quiet, friendly, alert, even-tempered, clever, sexy, intelligent

Life challenge for Rabbits To overcome a fear of change and take more risks in life.

The Rabbit lover The Rabbit is a fertile sign in China; this means that clandestine romance and intimate delights are the key indulgences of the amorous Rabbit. The symbol of fertility probably originates from Rabbits' physical attunement with nature and the cycles of life—they are highly sensitive to their own reproductive cycles. While they are generally passive lovers, Rabbits always practice discretion. They make lighthearted teasers who are attracted to older and wiser characters. Rabbits expect their intimate relationships to give them security and protection.

The Rabbit family member Rabbits make easygoing partners who relish the roles of homemaker and parent. Blessed with refinement and good taste, Rabbits can be meticulous about the decor and maintenance of their homes. Comfort is also a key need, and this ensures that everyone can feel relaxed in the Rabbit's home. Rabbits go to great lengths to ensure that harmonious relationships are maintained in the family, and they will not abide any tantrums or fighting on the part of their children and partners. They have a calming influence and like to practice what they preach.

The Rabbit friend Rabbits make caring and adaptable friends, whom others feel quite comfortable around at all times of day and night. Rabbits find the company of a few close friends reassuring and can prefer this to solitude. Hence, they will invest a lot of time in cultivating friendships. Their love of nature and curiosity about the world make them keen travelers and flexible traveling companions.

The Rabbit at work Rabbits prefer to work on their own in an evenly paced and calm environment. Independent occupations that can employ their good taste and refinement or kinship with the environment will feed their souls. Rabbits' intuition and wily intelligence equip them well, and the more gregarious of them, Fire Rabbits and Metal Rabbits, are suited to roles as diplomats or mediators. In the workplace, Rabbits' flexibility and genuine concern for others ensure that they can fit easily into any team. Provided the workplace is not marked by constant change and open hostility, Rabbits can perform well in numerous positions and types of businesses.

Ideal occupations for Rabbits Diplomat, antique dealer, interior decorator, art collector, biologist, sociologist, naturalist, forest ranger, counselor

The five Rabbit types

WOOD RABBITS • 1915, 1975 • The emphasis of double wood produces very generous, altruistic Rabbits who are preoccupied with receiving and sharing material wealth. Wood Rabbits are also quite creative and artistic and will often choose the arts to express their talents; they will also commit to frequent travel for inspiration.

FIRE RABBITS • 1927, 1987 • The presence of fire adds passion and more daring to the normally reticent Rabbit. Skilled with verbal dexterity, Fire Rabbits make great debaters and politicians who are not too fearful of the public eye when pursuing justice for minority groups. With their additional energy, Fire Rabbits also demonstrate more dedication to long-range plans than other Rabbits.

EARTH RABBITS • 1939, 1999 • The earth element adds to the Rabbit's already balanced nature, which means that Earth Rabbits are fairly pragmatic and moralistic. They are serious and hardworking characters who will follow tradition and apply caution when making decisions.

METAL RABBITS • 1951, 2011 • The metal element provides Rabbits with much-needed tenacity and courage. Metal Rabbits are the least emotional of all Rabbits and are adept in the political and business arena. They are also ambitious and will find much success, at least partly due to their intuitive skills. Metal Rabbits need to make sure that they do not become too rigid in their beliefs.

WATER RABBITS • 1963 • The water element deepens Rabbits' already intuitive and sensitive nature, making Water Rabbits extremely sensitive to their surroundings and others' hardships. Plagued by irrational fears and insecurity, Water Rabbits may become rather withdrawn and extremely passive; this will cause them to miss out on a lot of enjoyment in life.

Famous Rabbits

CARY GRANT, ACTOR

Cary Grant holds the title of the most debonair of all the matinee idols. His polished style, eloquence, and flawless manners are characteristic of the Water Rabbit and made him the most coveted romantic leading man during the 1930s, 1940s, and 1950s.

RELATIONSHIP CHART FOR RABBITS

Rabbit +	Rating	Potential for harmony in love, friendship, and professional life
Pig	Best friend	Both have peaceful and tolerant natures and will be able to provide each other with gentle, loving care. Pig will provide strength and openness, and Rabbit will provide practicality.
Sheep	Best friend	Both have loving and caring natures and will draw out and motivate each other. Rabbits will help Sheep set priorities for their responsibilities. Sheep will give Rabbits unconditional love.
Rat	Positive	A mutually rewarding partnership in most contexts. Both animals are highly intuitive and will be sympathetic toward each other and understanding of each other's needs.
Ox	Positive	Rabbit will be happy for Ox to dominate and provide. Rabbit's gentle optimism will act as a soothing balm to Ox's grueling pessimism.
Tiger	Positive	Flexible Rabbits will be happy for Tigers to take the lead. Tigers will feel appreciated and supported, and Rabbits will be encouraged to take bigger risks.
Rabbit	Good but needs work	A common understanding and calmness will ensure that there are few disagreements between these two. However, this union will be extremely passive and is likely to buckle under outside pressure.
Dragon	Challenging	Magnetic and impulsive Dragon will be too much for reserved and cautious Rabbit. Dragon will quickly tire of Rabbit's lack of strength.
Snake	Good but needs work	Their mutual tact and political correctness will keep these two respecting each other. Their secretive sides could lead to mutual suspicion if open communication is not maintained.
Horse	Challenging	Much frustration and misunderstanding will mark this pairing. Energetic and fiery Horse will lose patience with the steady pace and passivity of Rabbit.
Monkey	Challenging	Both are witty and inventive, which will ensure an attraction. However, Monkey will always be breaking social rules and norms, which Rabbit won't tolerate for long.
Dog	Good but needs work	Rabbits and Dogs have similar temperaments and are likely to put each other's needs before their own. While there will be little conflict, there will also be not much challenge between them, or much initiative taken.
Rooster	Archenemy	Roosters and Rabbits are poles apart in their values and social styles and, hence, little respect can be achieved. Rabbits are considerate and understated, and Roosters quite self-absorbed.

RAT

THE AMBITIOUS, INTELLIGENT RAT
1912, 1924, 1936, 1948, 1960, 1972, 1984, 1996, 2008
ENERGY: YANG
ELEMENT: WATER
TIME: 11:00 P.M.–1:00 A.M.
MONTH: DECEMBER
DIRECTION: NORTH
SEASON: WINTER

Rats are the resourceful masterminds of the Chinese zodiac. Highly communicative and endowed with abundant intelligence and financial acumen, they are driven by the desire to accumulate wealth and so ensure their financial security.

Their superior analytical skills guarantee them career success. They make excellent strategic partners in business, where they are motivated just as much by accolades as they are by financial reward.

Being social creatures, Rats are at home in groups. They love to entertain and maintain active social diaries. They are perceived by their friends as both tasteful and elegant, in an understated way. Given sufficient praise and applause from loved ones, Rats make loyal, protective, and committed partners and family members.

The Rat ascendant for those born between 11:00 P.M. and 1:00 A.M.

The Rat as the ascendant sign stimulates the mental aspects of the personality and boosts both social charms and communication skills.

Rats at their best Intelligent, accomplished, charming, innovative, loyal, empathic, ambitious

Rats at their worst Secretive, anxious, calculating, possessive, stingy, excessive, neurotic, critical, egotistical

Character traits of Rats Intelligent, industrious, resourceful, practical, self-motivated, thrifty, charming, communicative, compassionate, calm, observant, analytical, caring, discreet

---

Rats are chiefly concerned with power and material security. Ambition, success, and accumulation of wealth feature in their lives. Aided by their innate analytical skills, they can devise elaborate plans that are assured of great success. Rats embody entrepreneurial and leadership skills.

Life challenge for Rats To overcome their inner fears and insecurities and reduce their nervous anxiety.

The Rat lover Well equipped with quick wits, warm natures, and stylish grooming, Rats have great success as attentive and debonair lovers. While young, they are drawn to the challenge of artful seduction using their extensive interpersonal skills. However, it is the quality of a committed, long-term relationship they desire most, not a lifelong parade of superficial affairs. Once committed, they make gentle, loyal, and protective partners who will always take time out to nurture their relationships and support and care for their partners. Rats' craving for their partners' approval and adoration will deter most from straying. Rats are not by nature promiscuous.

The Rat family member Rats make ideal providers for and protectors of their families. Rats take their family responsibilities seriously, and relish the roles of breadwinner and caretaker. As born leaders, they will want to be the more dominant partner, especially in decision making. While practicality and thrift will be themes in their households, Rats are able to balance this with emotional warmth and sensitivity to those they love. Rats make considerate parents and fine role models who will take an active part in their children's upbringing.

The Rat friend Rats are also loyal to others they care about. Rats will prefer a few close and supportive friendships to numerous acquaintances and are likely to keep childhood friendships for life. Rats love to be admired and respected and will seek opportunities to give their friends advice. They make dependable, supportive, and sincere friends, and love to entertain in small numbers, especially where food is involved. They often hold fabulous dinner parties.

The Rat at work To remain stimulated, Rats need to be continually challenged intellectually in their work. Without adequate amounts of praise and recognition, Rats can become insecure and unmotivated. This causes them to become restless and move from one job to the next. As the "rat race" is their domain, they usually find the ride to the director's suite an easy trip, enjoying much success in their professional lives. To their colleagues, Rats appear competent and emotionally self-contained, sometimes even a little secretive.

Ideal occupations for Rats Business director, accountant, stockbroker, courtroom lawyer, auctioneer, politician

The five Rat types

WOOD RATS • 1924, 1984 • The wood element heightens some core character traits in this Rat. Wood Rats are even more hardworking and anxious than other Rats. They hesitate when making decisions, preferring to gather lots of information and take plenty of time to assess the situation before making a move.

FIRE RATS • 1936, 1996 • Fire brings passion and burning enthusiasm to the Rat. Fire Rats are witty and charming, which adds to their already healthy dose of personal appeal. They are not above heroic deeds to impress a loved one and can always attract an admiring crowd.

EARTH RATS • 1948, 2008 • Earth provides Rats with a good helping of practicality and wisdom. Earth Rats are the "old souls" of the Rat family. Their careful advice and wise counsel are their distinguishing features. Contrary to the usual traits of Rats, Earth Rats actually enjoy their own company.

METAL RATS • 1960 • Metal lends Rats a good dose of physical and mental strength. Metal Rats can have fixed ideas and can appear stubborn. Metal Rats are the most professionally successful of Rats, and usually do well as entrepreneurs.

WATER RATS • 1912, 1972 • Water is the Rat's natural element, so Water Rats have increased communication skills. They are gifted communicators and have an abundance of public appeal; they usually seek out public positions and have the potential to be great orators or writers.

Famous Rats

GEORGE WASHINGTON, FIRST PRESIDENT OF THE UNITED STATES

George Washington demonstrated great oratory skills and had wide public appeal—traits specifically associated with Water Rats.

MATA HARI, SPY

Mata Hari was a world-famous spy for Germany during the first World War. A skilled seductress, she displayed the wit and charm for which Fire Rats are famous. She was able to obtain highly confidential military secrets from her intimate relationships with high-ranking Allied officers.

RELATIONSHIP CHART FOR RATS

Rat +	Rating	Potential for harmony in love, friendship, and professional life
Monkey	Best friend	Each will admire the other's quick wit and superior intelligence. Provided Rat remains tolerant of Monkey's antics, these two will initiate many schemes and ingenious plans together.
Dragon	Best friend	Both are charged with energy and social charisma, and this will keep them satisfied. Each will be intuitive about the other's unspoken desires and will be able to meet the other's needs.
Rat	Good but needs work	Good compatibility, particularly for business or friendships. Each will respect and understand the other, but unless the couple has a busy lifestyle, boredom will quickly set in.
Ox	Positive	A mutually rewarding partnership in any context. Rat's intelligence and ingenuity will complement Ox's physical tenacity. This pair could achieve much together.
Tiger	Challenging	They have different perspectives on life and clashing personal values and goals. Any attraction will be only fleeting, with Rat more interested in material accumulation and Tiger in adventure.
Rabbit	Positive	A mutually rewarding partnership in most contexts. Both animals are highly intuitive and will be sympathetic toward each other and understanding of each other's needs.
Snake	Positive	Each will challenge the other's mental prowess, ensuring that a satisfying relationship evolves where each can learn much from the other.
Sheep	Challenging	Interest in each other will be only fleeting and marginally rewarding. The Rat will need more than just Sheep's adoring devotion to maintain interest, and Sheep will feel hurt by Rat's dwindling attention.
Rooster	Challenging	Each will be too quick to misjudge the other. Rat will view Rooster as too flamboyant and superficial, and Rooster will lose patience with Rat's cool and collected exterior.
Dog	Good but needs work	This pairing can work if kept at friendship level. Both signs are nagged by personal insecurities, which will accumulate with the pairing. Dog will misinterpret Rat's secrecy as underhanded scheming.
Pig	Good but needs work	The sensuous Pig will revel in Rat's material acquisitions. Rat will at first enjoy its provider role and will then be likely to take Pig for granted; there is little hope for long-term success.
Horse	Archenemy	Both have healthy egos, which will be bruised regularly in this pairing. Horse will want physical and verbal freedom, a request that the politically correct Rat will be loath to respect.

RAVEN

Ravens, as black as night itself, are said by Native Americans to possess magical powers; sighting one is a message to turn and face your inner darkness and fears, and transform your life.

Raven people are extraordinarily special individuals, as they act as natural catalysts for the transformation of other people's lives. To achieve this, they are especially intuitive and diplomatic, demonstrating great care and consideration for their fellow humans. They are generally openhearted, charming, peace-loving people who demonstrate exceptional communication skills,

particularly in terms of listening.

Ravens have a strong social conscience, which can lead them to be overly idealistic at times. As they are good at starting things, you will often find them working tirelessly behind the scenes to influence those in power, getting them to restore and maintain harmony and peace within their communities.

Raven people tend to dislike solitude, preferring the company of others, whether in a social, business, or personal context.

SEASON	Early fall—a time of browning and falling leaves, shortening days
SEASON TOTEM	Grizzly Bear
SEASON ELEMENT	Earth
BIRTH TIME	September 23–October 22 Northern Hemisphere March 21–April 19 Southern Hemisphere
BIRTH TIME ELEMENT	Air
ELEMENTAL CLAN	Butterfly
ENERGY FLOW	Active
AFFINITIES	Color: brown Plant: mullein Mineral: bloodstone jasper
GIFTS	Intelligence, insight, intuition, inspiration, diplomacy, influence, adaptability, resourcefulness
CHALLENGES	Depression, indecision, confusion, manipulativeness
LIFE PATH	To explore and comprehend humans' inner darkness and then to act as the communication medium between the physical and spiritual worlds for others.

Physically attractive and affectionate, they need to give and receive physical affection regularly; if they do not, they may slip into a depressive or confused emotional state.

At their best, Ravens are quite in tune with their physical and emotional sides. This leaves only one real challenge—to develop their latent psychic abilities. If they do this, they can be of much greater service to others as healers or as psychic mediums.

IDEAL PAIRINGS	
Raven +	Relationship potential
Otter	Both have strong humanitarian values and will find in each other the support and encouragement they require.
Deer	This pair will exude grace and charm. They are both active and will be quite communicative with each other.
Salmon	Intuitive Raven will supply energetic Salmon with clear direction. Salmon will provide Raven with the determination and courage needed for pursuing goals.
Owl	Sensible Owl will encourage Raven's strong social conscience. Raven will reward Owl with influential networks and contacts.
Hawk	**Complement.** A natural attraction and kinship exists between these two animal totems. Each will make the other a loyal and supportive companion.

CHALLENGING PAIRINGS	
Raven +	Relationship potential
Snow Goose	Serious and authoritative Snow Goose will not be able to lift Raven's occasional depression. Snow Goose will see no value in the union.
Wolf	As neither are capable of making decisions in a relationship, nothing will be achieved. This could open the door to depression for both.
Beaver	Influential Raven achieves success through others, while Beaver achieves success through sheer hard work. There will be no appreciation for each other's tactics.
Woodpecker	Woodpecker will be too sensitive and vulnerable to Raven's confusion and indecision. Raven will find Woodpecker lacking in energy and inspiration.
Brown Bear	Brown Bear will grow critical of Raven's idealistic goals and charitable inclinations. Raven will find Brown Bear lacking in enthusiasm.
Snake	Raven will be open to manipulation and deception when Snake turns on the charisma. But Snake will soon tire of the game, and Raven will feel lucky to be out of the union.
Raven	Raven pairing with another will bring about a mirroring effect, whereby the best and the worst in each other will be magnified.

ROOSTER

THE ALERT, HONORABLE ROOSTER
1921, 1933, 1945, 1957, 1969, 1981, 1993, 2005, 2017
ENERGY: YIN
ELEMENT: METAL
TIME: 5:00 P.M.–7:00 P.M.
MONTH: SEPTEMBER
DIRECTION: WEST
SEASON: FALL

Roosters are spirited, fearless, proud individuals who speak their minds and are meticulous in their dress. They are flashy, jumping at every opportunity to socialize and entertain. Desiring the limelight, they love being center stage.

As they are so keen on appearances, Roosters can be overly sensitive to the criticism of others. Underneath all the bright feathers, they are extremely intelligent. Blessed with acute perception and a yearning for knowledge, they are scrupulous in their attention to detail and have extraordinarily high standards. A Rooster's life is anything but dull.

The Rooster ascendant for those born between 5:00 P.M. and 7:00 P.M.

The Rooster as the ascendant sign ensures integrity and a sense of honor. Roosters are keenly alert and quick to voice their opinions.

Roosters at their best Alert, cultivated, direct, entertaining, expressive, knowledgeable, meticulous, resourceful, resilient

Roosters at their worst Vulnerable, critical, proud, frank, argumentative, impulsive, vain, selfish, pretentious

Character traits of Roosters Flamboyant, resourceful, courageous, resilient, cultivated, capable, entertaining, critical, proud, knowledgeable, ambitious, frank, extravagant, protective, impulsive, provocative

Rooster's tenth position at Buddha's side denotes strength, alertness, and honor—usually military honor. Roosters are flamboyant people who are attracted to pomp and ceremony in social occasions. Appearances mean everything to Roosters, who spend much time on their looks and prefer to be admired more for their appearance than for their intelligence.

Life challenge for Roosters To believe truly in themselves and rely less on others' opinions.

The Rooster lover Rooster lovers need to be the boss—they must be in control of all of their relationships. Every love affair will be conducted on their terms, and should their partners oblige, Roosters will generously reward them with expensive dinners, fine wine, exotic holidays, and lavish presents.

As appearances mean everything, Roosters will put a lot of energy into their sexual performance and may be critical of their partners. To win their hearts and soften their exterior armor, the frequent use of flattery and lavish praise is essential.

The Rooster family member Roosters have high expectations of their partners and children and want them to shine in any social gathering. Hence Roosters can be demanding and not the easiest to live with. However, they are generous in the extreme and will protect their families and homes to the death if need be. The Rooster child displays these same traits and is also a keen reader who shows scholastic potential. Roosters can make a vibrant addition to any family, as long as they have a special place in their home where they can relax and collect their wits, and their family members learn to not be offended by their occasional blasts of hot wind.

The Rooster friend Roosters love to entertain—they will go all out with dress, catering, and furnishings to impress their guests. Addicted to compliments, Roosters will put much energy into decorating their homes with the latest styles and may be obsessed with cleanliness. As Roosters like to be held in high esteem by their friends, they are generous with their time and possessions. In their much-needed quiet time, Roosters will indulge their private passion for reading.

The Rooster at work Roosters' love of ceremony and tradition will see them attracted to professional careers in the military or the police force. In fact, any profession that requires a uniform will seem impressive and dramatic to the Rooster. Roosters work hard and attend to details so that they can receive the accolades that a job well done will bring them; they will not necessarily receive much pleasure from the work itself. Articulate and knowledgeable,

Roosters know how to gain attention and will not go unnoticed in any work environment. Therefore, professions that provide them with a lot of attention will suit them.

Ideal occupations for Roosters TV show host, military officer, public relations officer, salesperson, critic, academic, actor, model

The five Rooster types

WOOD ROOSTERS • 1945, 2005 • The wood element provides Roosters with the opportunity to gain wisdom throughout their lives. Wood Roosters are less hot-tempered and more easygoing than the average Rooster and will prefer spending their time in quiet pursuit of knowledge.

FIRE ROOSTERS • 1957, 2017 • Fire adds more heat to Roosters' already passionate and daring personality. Fire Roosters are bold in both dress and manner. They have presence and, as they are not swayed much by others' opinions, can attain high public positions.

EARTH ROOSTERS • 1969 • The earth element ensures that these Roosters are more grounded than other Roosters. Earth Roosters are not as flamboyant or argumentative. As they are more self-controlled, they have more ability to manage their personal finances.

METAL ROOSTERS • 1921, 1981 • The effect of double metal is to make Roosters even more resolute and uncompromising in manner. Metal Roosters are perfectionists who set high standards for themselves and others. Supercritical of everything and everyone, they may be difficult to get along with.

WATER ROOSTERS • 1933, 1993 • Water provides Roosters with more personal adaptability and more empathy for others. Water Roosters enjoy their social activities and are attractive to a wider audience. Less self-obsessed than other Roosters, Water Roosters are a pleasure to have around.

Famous Roosters

PETER USTINOV, ACTOR/PRODUCER/WRITER

Peter Ustinov is a fine example of Roosters' love of pomp and ceremony. As a Metal Rooster, he can be headstrong and particular in his work. His acting and writing display his vibrant disposition.

JOAN COLLINS, ACTOR

A typical Water Rooster, Joan Collins loves social activities, portraying the role of rich, immaculate social queen to perfection. Dripping in diamonds and clothed in nothing but high fashion, she automatically lights up every socially significant occasion, clearly displaying the Water Rooster traits.

RELATIONSHIP CHART FOR ROOSTERS

Rooster +	Rating	Potential for harmony in love, friendship, and professional life
Ox	Best friend	Much success could come from this pairing, as flamboyant Rooster will attend to the social aspects of the relationship, while Ox will attend to the detailed planning and physical work.
Snake	Best friend	Each will complement and have respect for the other. Snake will admire Rooster's flamboyant social presence, and Rooster will appreciate Snake's wise counsel and social refinement.
Rat	Challenging	Each will be too quick to misjudge the other. Rat will view Rooster as too flamboyant and superficial, while Rooster will lose patience with Rat's cool and controlled exterior.
Tiger	Good but needs work	Each will be attracted to the other's appearance, but Rooster and Tiger will have very different communication styles. Rooster will henpeck Tiger on every detail, which will frustrate carefree Tiger.
Dragon	Good but needs work	Mutual attraction is assured, as Dragon and Rooster regularly share the limelight. Unfortunately, neither will be very interested in a committed relationship with the other.
Horse	Good but needs work	Both are lively and entertaining, which ensures initial attraction. However, Rooster will want to control the relationship, which will cause Horse to bolt.
Sheep	Challenging	Each suffers from personal insecurities, which will make this an unproductive pairing. Rooster will not be able to understand Sheep's introversion. Sheep will feel embarrassed by Rooster's flamboyance.
Monkey	Positive	There is a lot of potential with this pairing, as both are lively entertainers. Both will need to restrain themselves from judging the other too quickly to ensure that they see all the qualities the other offers.
Rooster	Good but needs work	An exotic and attractive pairing, these two will maintain an extensive social life. As each will fight for control, they will need to exercise restraint and understanding.
Dog	Challenging	These two have different values and beliefs. Dog will find Rooster egotistical and self-absorbed, and Rooster will find Dog too moralistic and unselfish for his or her own good.
Pig	Positive	Pig will be happy for Rooster to rule and will be understanding of Rooster's secret insecurities. Rooster will appreciate Pig's support and will reward Pig with its generosity.
Rabbit	Archenemy	The Rooster and the Rabbit are poles apart in their values and social styles and, hence, there will be little respect between them. Rabbit is considerate and understated, and Rooster is fairly self-absorbed.

S

SAGITTARIUS

NOVEMBER 23 TO DECEMBER 21
SYMBOL: THE ARCHER
RULING PLANET: JUPITER
GROUPS: POSITIVE, FIRE, MUTABLE

Most of you are outgoing, generous, humorous, and enthusiastic, but not all are like this. For Sagittarians, the biggest challenge is often a sense of restlessness that interferes with their focus. You may sometimes feel that you are too scattered. It is important for you to set goals and to incorporate activities, such as exercise, that will help you release your restlessness in your day. Playing sports and being outdoors holds particular appeal to Sagittarians—these activities help them cope with any feeling of restriction and allow them to have a challenge to conquer.

You enjoy large projects, and many of you are excellent builders and handypersons. Sagittarians have a strong intellect and are interested in working on a large scale. Their ambition has led to a number of Sagittarians being noted for acquiring a vast empire or gaining worldwide recognition—Walt Disney and Frank Sinatra are good examples. Publishing and teaching are other areas in which a Sagittarian can excel.

You prefer a skilled type of job that takes you from place to place and in which you meet a number of different people. You particularly need work that is not too predictable. Acting is one

---

ASTROLOGICAL COMPATIBILITY

WHAT SUN SIGN ARE YOU? Sagittarius

WHO ARE YOUR FRIENDS? Libra, Aquarius

WHO ARE YOUR LOVERS? Aries, Leo

---

career choice that appeals to Sagittarians—Douglas Fairbanks Jr., Sammy Davis Jr., and Kirk Douglas were all Sagittarians.

Being restless, you love to travel and you may actually end up living in a different country from the one in which you were born. Travel often encourages Sagittarians to learn the new country's language, and they enjoy the challenge of communicating with the locals in their own tongue.

Sagittarians enjoy the opportunity to learn new things. They are particularly gifted in research skills and love gathering information. Some Sagittarians have channeled this into literary works—famous Sagittarians include the novelists Mark Twain and Jane Austen, and the poet William Blake.

Some of you are quiet and introspective, and you can all confuse a lover by your sudden lapses into silence and your lack of feedback. However, these lapses do not last for long—your interest in a situation or person is quickly rekindled, reviving your famous enthusiasm. Overly introspective behavior may come from a feeling of physical restriction or a sense of claustrophobia in a relationship.

It would be wise to talk to your partner to figure out what you can do about this.

Sometimes your ambition may get in the way of your family life, but you adore your family and take special interest in your children's education. Your great enthusiasm for life and your ability to share information makes you an excellent teacher for your children.

You can be extremely generous and helpful to your partner. For a marriage partner, you need to find someone who shares your interests and enthusiasms. You generally do not like planning in advance, instead preferring to allow surprises to come into your life.

You prefer to live in an open-plan house where there is a casual flow of energy and where you can feel comfortable. Your sense of casualness is also evident in the way you dress, as you choose garments that are comfortable rather than those that restrict your movement.

SALMON

In the wild, salmon are required to swim back upstream, against the rushing tide, to find their spawning grounds. Native Americans respect them for their vital energy and determination. Seeing salmon make their trek upstream is a reminder to us to take stock of our own vital energies and to ensure that they are kept in control and directed positively.

Salmon people are outgoing, action-oriented people who find it difficult to slow their hectic daily pace. They are robust and usually look larger than life. Gregarious and versatile, they are bombastic when communicating. At the very least, Salmon people always stand out in a crowd.

At their best, Salmon are friendly and charming, never failing to entertain in social settings. At their worst, they can be erratic, even impulsive, and hot-tempered and almost vengeful if they allow their emotions to run unchecked.

When the situation calls for courage, Salmon are usually first in line. This makes them naturally suited to leadership roles, where

SEASON	Heart of summer—a time of ripening, of reaching growth potential
SEASON TOTEM	Coyote
SEASON ELEMENT	Water
BIRTH TIME	July 23–August 22 Northern Hemisphere January 20–February 18 Southern Hemisphere
BIRTH TIME ELEMENT	Fire
ELEMENTAL CLAN	Thunderbird
ENERGY FLOW	Active
AFFINITIES	Color: red Plant: raspberry Mineral: garnet
GIFTS	Energy, versatility, sensuality, benevolence, determination, affection, charm, courage
CHALLENGES	Impulsiveness, arrogance, selfishness, greed
LIFE PATH	To harness the vital energies that can surge through you, in order to achieve emotional balance and harmony with your environment.

their bighearted and magnanimous approach to others can be widely appreciated.

Salmon people are also sensual. They take pride in their outward appearance and even more in their sexual prowess. They sometimes need to curb their personal desires in order to ensure that selfishness and greed do not take control of their actions and in the process misdirect their honor and integrity.

IDEAL PAIRINGS	
Salmon +	*Relationship potential*
Owl	Both have energy to burn and will find the other stimulating company. Salmon can gain wise counsel from Owl, while Owl will find Salmon has an exciting charm.
Hawk	Both have high energy. Hawk will provide the ideas and foresight, while Salmon will provide the determination necessary for enacting all plans.
Deer	Both are versatile and this will be mutually attractive. Deer will be happy to be directed by the determined Salmon, who will bestow much affection on Deer.
Raven	Intuitive Raven will supply energetic Salmon with clear direction. Salmon will provide Raven with the determination and courage needed for pursuing goals.
Otter	**Complement.** A natural attraction and kinship exists between these two animal totems. Each will make the other a loyal and supportive companion.

CHALLENGING PAIRINGS	
Salmon +	*Relationship potential*
Snow Goose	Both have extremely healthy egos, which will make it difficult for either to compromise.
Wolf	Salmon is likely to take advantage of Wolf's trusting heart. Wolf will soon leave the relationship wounded and depressed.
Beaver	Salmon will want excitement and sensual stimulation from Beaver, and Beaver will want practicality and endeavor. Both will end up empty-handed.
Woodpecker	Woodpeckers like to stay at home and cuddle, while Salmon would rather go out and party. Each will go their own way in time.
Brown Bear	Cheerful Salmon will not be impressed with Brown Bear's cynicism, and Brown Bear will be too critical of Salmon's wayward charm and sensuality.
Snake	Both are quite sensual, but Salmon is openly affectionate, while Snake will only demonstrate feelings in private. Over time, they will come to feel uncomfortable in each other's company.
Salmon	Salmon pairing with another will bring about a mirroring effect, whereby the best and the worst in each other will be magnified.

SCORPIO

OCTOBER 24 TO NOVEMBER 22
SYMBOL: THE SCORPION
RULING PLANET: PLUTO
GROUPS: NEGATIVE, WATER, FIXED

You have a mixture of characteristics, and there are times when you can switch between personalities. You can be quite extroverted at times, as well as hotheaded, ambitious, and intolerant of obstacles. At other times, you may be introverted and shy, taking a long time to trust a person.

Scorpios will take their time to make a decision about their path in life or their life's partner. However, when they finally commit, they will make a success of their career and will be extremely passionate with their partner.

Concerning your work life, for most of the time you are reasonable, hardworking, sensible, intelligent, humorous, and loving, but you can turn into a critical control freak if you are not careful. Your challenge is to trust in your work colleagues and not succumb to your inclination to feel undermined and suspicious.

You are a hard and reliable worker, but you prefer to be the power behind the throne than to sit on it yourself. Famous Scorpians include Leon Trotsky, Robert Kennedy, and Indira Gandhi. In business, you would rather stay in the office than meet with clients and network with those in your industry.

You can be quite competitive, which can get you a long way in your career, and if you can channel it into sports or some other activity, you can achieve considerable success and enjoy yourself at the same time. Overly aggressive behavior can be a problem for Scorpios, especially when they feel frustrated or unhappy. An inherent sense of humor can be used to help defuse the accumulation of anger over a long period of time.

Scorpios are particularly adept at making money, no matter what venture they engage in. You have excellent business sense and can excel in areas that require a great deal of study and investigation, such as law, finance, or medicine.

You are extremely loyal to those you love, especially your children, and you always want the best for them. However, if you have been crossed by one you love, you tend to be unforgiving. The challenge for Scorpios is to not withdraw but to give their

partner, friend, or colleague a chance to explain their behavior, to find some resolution to the situation. Consequently, life with a Scorpio can be full of passionate highs and stormy lows—it is never dull!

Scorpios are also particularly adept at helping their children and their partners make the most of their lives, although sometimes Scorpios can become intolerant when their loved ones miss or do not properly make use of their opportunities.

You tend to enjoy living near water and you will like a home environment that is filled with the tools and books you need to study in peace and quiet.

ASTROLOGICAL COMPATIBILITY

♏

WHAT SUN SIGN ARE YOU? Scorpio

WHO ARE YOUR FRIENDS? Virgo, Capricorn

WHO ARE YOUR LOVERS? Cancer, Pisces

SEPTEMBER

SEPTEMBER ~ VIRGO
FROM THE 1ST TO THE 22ND

The earth sign of Virgo signifies a quick mind and a talent for research and analysis, but it can make you too concerned with details. Your Chinese astrology receptive metal element adds ambition and an innovative mind, and it draws you toward the world of show business and the arts. The sign of the Rooster adds even more glamour, plus honesty, but it also means you have a tendency to brag about your achievements.

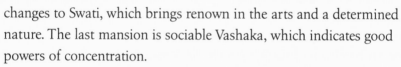

Your Vedic sign is Simha, which is noted for generosity and a love of children and family life. The first Vedic mansion is Chitra, which can lead to success and an interest in the arts and sciences. This soon changes to Swati, which brings renown in the arts and a determined nature. The last mansion is sociable Vashaka, which indicates good powers of concentration.

The Native American Brown Bear of the Turtle clan signifies intelligence, curiosity, a realistic attitude, and a sense of humor. The West African sign of the Kola Nut can make you changeable, but it also brings intuition, which helps you make wise decisions. This changes to the Traveler, which can indicate either physical travel or the ability to move between the real world and the spiritual world.

The first Celtic tree sign is Pine, which indicates passionate feelings that are hidden within your reserved outer nature. This is

followed by the Willow, which signifies intuition and a love of anything mysterious. The final Celtic tree sign is the Lime, which denotes ambition and great organizing skills on the outside and a soft heart within. The Norse runic sign is Raidho, which suggests a traveler who gains wisdom along the way. It then changes to Kaunaz, the sign of the inventor.

SEPTEMBER ~ LIBRA

FROM THE 23RD ONWARD

The air sign of Libra is responsible for your kind heart and your artistic nature. Librans can dither and find it hard to make decisions, but once they have set their mind on something, they usually make a success of it. The Chinese Rooster suggests a wonderful sense of humor and friendliness, but it can also make you opinionated. The receptive metal element draws you to the world of the arts or the glamour of show business.

The Vedic sign of Simha adds to your desire to be around glittering and glamorous people, but this soon changes to the more serious and literary sign of Kanya, which denotes an analytical mind. The mansion of Vashaka makes you clever and pleasant, and it suggests that you have the power to overcome obstacles in life; you can also become a powerful enemy to those who hurt you.

The Native American Raven of the Butterfly clan ensures that you are kind, loving, and helpful to others, and that your powers of intuition are particularly strong. Being a Butterfly, you can jump from one idea to the next. The West African sign of the Traveler might take you on actual journeys; it might also help you reach into spiritual realms and back again into the earthly plane.

The Celtic tree sign of the Olive is noted for intelligence, a balanced mind, and a certain charisma. This changes to the Hazel, which indicates charm and also nervous restlessness. The Norse

runic sign of Kaunaz leads you to make discoveries and to explore the world of ideas, even if you have to stay up all night to do so. The last day of September belongs to Gebo, which denotes generosity and a helpful nature.

SHEEP

THE SERENE, PEACEFUL SHEEP
1919, 1931, 1943, 1955, 1967, 1979, 1991, 2003, 2015
ENERGY: YIN
ELEMENT: EARTH
TIME: 1:00 P.M.–3:00 P.M.
MONTH: JULY
DIRECTION: SOUTH/SOUTHWEST
SEASON: LATE SUMMER

Sheep are the peacemakers of the Chinese zodiac. Calm by nature, they are pacifists and will recoil from any confrontation. They are also quiet, friendly, patient, extremely adaptable, and get along with others very easily. They make good listeners and are sympathetic friends.

Highly principled, sensitive, and artistically talented, sheep will often find their calling in the fields of music, literature, or art. Here they revel in being left alone, free of the influence of others, to express their imagination.

The Sheep ascendant for those born between 1:00 P.M. and 3:00 P.M.

Having the Sheep as the ascendant sign will add peace and serenity. People with this ascendant sign may be flexible and lighthearted.

Sheep at their best Adaptable, considerate, compassionate, creative, easygoing, gentle, sincere, careful

Sheep at their worst Eccentric, vulnerable, sensitive, pessimistic, naive, gullible, self-indulgent, irresponsible

Character traits of Sheep Creative, imaginative, sensitive, sincere, cautious, adaptable, gentle, easygoing, refined, moderate, calm, optimistic, orderly, friendly, romantic, sympathetic, pleasant, honest

Life challenge for Sheep To develop confidence in their own abilities and to take more risks in life.

> Sheep's eighth position at Buddha's side is associated with peace and serenity. Sheep are introverts, and are quiet, patient, and quite friendly. Extreme pacifists, they detest violence in any form. They live by their strong values and beliefs, and have a keen sense of right and wrong.

The Sheep lover Sheep are very sexy people who are intuitively aware of their partner's and their own sexual natures. This is a fertile sign. Sheep are romantic, caring, and sensitive lovers who will want to experience many partners before settling down. While Sheep can be a little self-conscious about their bodies and big sexual appetites, they are not so quiet as to let their needs go unfulfilled. Sheep will let you know tactfully exactly what makes them happy. Once committed, Sheep make faithful and considerate partners.

The Sheep family member The security and stability of family life suits Sheep, and can act as a source of inspiration and support to fuel their creative talents.

Nostalgic in the extreme, Sheep will fill their homes with family photos and display many mementos of their families' important occasions. Sheep make considerate and easygoing partners and patient, nurturing parents. They are able to maintain good communication and close ties with their children. Sheep are the peacemakers in their families, and they strive to keep their home environment harmonious.

The Sheep friend Kindhearted and generous of spirit, Sheep make very understanding friends who will stick by their pals through thick and thin. It is the Sheep friend to whom all turn for a shoulder to cry on and a sympathetic ear. Sheep are nonjudgmental and find it easy to forgive. While they like to socialize and are very good at bringing people together, Sheep frequently need time alone to rest and rejuvenate.

The Sheep at work Sheep are much liked by their employers and colleagues, who find them friendly, and are very good with detail and with analytical work. Sheep may be particular with their own work and others may perceive them as perfectionists. Sheep need a supportive, stress-free work environment in order to perform and frequently fall ill if their workplace becomes chaotic.

If they pursue their artistic talents, they need a degree of freedom to allow their imaginations to wander unhindered. Not overly ambitious in the traditional sense, Sheep are motivated not by money or power, but by creative license and the enjoyment of happy relationships.

Ideal occupations for Sheep Writer, poet, musician, artist, actor, therapist, religious minister, architect, gardener

The five Sheep types

WOOD SHEEP • 1955, 2015 • Wood strengthens Sheep's creative talents, so Wood Sheep usually end up as humble artists or musicians. Wood Sheep are also very compassionate and generous people and have a large number of friends.

FIRE SHEEP • 1967 • Fire adds some passion and energy to the normally reserved and patient Sheep. Fire Sheep are more confident in their own abilities than other Sheep and use their personal charm to get what they want from others.

EARTH SHEEP • 1919, 1979 • The effect of double earth on the Sheep character is to heighten all its inherent traits. Earth Sheep are shining examples of strong moral beliefs. Many Earth Sheep are deeply spiritual and are attracted to religious or missionary work as a career.

METAL SHEEP • 1931, 1991 • Metal strengthens the Sheep character. Metal Sheep display a more forthright and determined side to their personalities than most Sheep and have no trouble persevering, despite all manner of obstacles, in order to achieve their desires.

WATER SHEEP • 1943, 2003 • Water heightens Sheep emotions and intuition. Water Sheep are supersensitive to everyone and everything around them, which can cause them to be highly stressed and anxious individuals. Water Sheep are advised to undertake a lot of self-development and relaxation courses.

Famous Sheep

JOHN DENVER, SINGER/SONGWRITER

Denver displayed the typical creative and peaceful mind of the Sheep with his songs of love and nature. Also an environmentalist, John Denver was able to relieve his stress and achieve emotional balance by spending much of his time in the Rocky Mountains.

MARGOT FONTEYN, BALLERINA

Fonteyn followed her artistic calling—such a calling is present in many Sheep—and achieved worldwide acclaim as a ballerina. The presence of the double earth element ensured that she was able to stay focused on her dance technique and to adapt herself easily to any dance role.

RELATIONSHIP CHART FOR SHEEP

Sheep +	Rating	Potential for harmony in love, friendship, and professional life
Rabbit	Best friend	Both have loving and caring natures and will draw out and motivate each other. Rabbits will help Sheep set priorities for their responsibilities. Sheep will give Rabbits unconditional love.
Pig	Best friend	Both are sensitive and understanding and will be supportive of each other. The environment will be so tranquil that their creative talents will flourish.
Rat	Challenging	Interest in each other will be only fleeting and marginally rewarding. Rat will need more than just Sheep's adoring devotion in order to maintain interest, and Sheep will feel hurt by Rat's dwindling attention.
Tiger	Good but needs work	Apart from their high sex drives, Tiger and Sheep will have little else in common. Sheep will be hurt by Tiger's need for adventure and personal space. Tiger will soon feel that the relationship is claustrophobic.
Dragon	Challenging	This pair are stark opposites and will struggle to find anything in common or to appreciate anything in the other. Dragon will demand adventure, while Sheep will want stability.
Snake	Good but needs work	There is enough mutual interest in art, music, and theater for these two to be friends. However, Sheep is quite sentimental and sensitive and will soon be put off by Snake's detachment.
Horse	Positive	These two will have much in common, especially creative ability, which they will encourage and help develop in each other. The only hurdle will be the Horse's lack of commitment.
Sheep	Good but needs work	This relationship will be warm and even-tempered, as neither will want to offend the other. However, at least one of them will need to take care of the practical side of their lives if they are to survive.
Monkey	Positive	Monkeys will soon have Sheep laughing at themselves and more willing to take risks, while Sheep will instill some morals in Monkeys and curb their excesses.
Rooster	Challenging	Each suffers from personal insecurities, which will make this an unproductive pairing. Rooster will not be able to understand Sheep's introversion. Sheep will feel embarrassed by Rooster's flamboyance.
Dog	Positive	As both are very tolerant, these two will be able to understand and appreciate each other's differences. Dog will generally find Sheep a moral ally. Sheep will appreciate Dog's protection.
Ox	Archenemy	Ox will have no respect for Sheep, and Sheep will find no excitement in Ox. This pairing is best avoided, as the values and beliefs of the two will be directly opposed.

SNAKE (CHINESE)

THE WISE, INFLUENTIAL SNAKE
1917, 1929, 1941, 1953, 1965, 1977, 1989, 2001, 2013
ENERGY: YIN
ELEMENT: FIRE
TIME: 9:00 A.M.–11:00 A.M.
MONTH: MAY
DIRECTION: SOUTH/SOUTHEAST
SEASON: EARLY SUMMER

In China, snakes are admired for their beauty and wisdom. Snake people have a serene presence, and rarely reveal feelings of agitation or stress. Self-disciplined and tradition-loving, they are thinkers rather than doers.

Given their perceptive minds, natural sophistication, and reflective natures, Snakes are often sought after for their opinions and counsel. They make skilled negotiators and will swiftly distinguish themselves in any position of influence.

The Snake ascendant for those born between 9:00 A.M. and 11:00 A.M.

Having the Snake as the ascendant sign gives rise to reflection on the self, objectivity, and wisdom. Snakes radiate sexuality and attractiveness.

Snakes at their best Discreet, enticing, intelligent, enigmatic, wise, refined, sensual, instinctive, methodical, shrewd, perceptive

Snakes at their worst Calculating, vengeful, lazy, suspicious, jealous, extravagant, standoffish, possessive, fickle

Character traits of Snakes Alert, intelligent, intuitive, wise, calculating, conservative, cautious, mysterious, alluring, elegant, shrewd, sophisticated, sensual, reflective, organized

Life challenge for Snakes To become more physically involved in their world and more emotionally accessible.

The Snake lover The alluring Snakes are gifted seducers, able to

Snake's sixth position at Buddha's side denotes centrality and wisdom; it is a position of quiet but distinct influence. Snakes are able to draw strength and power effortlessly from those around them. Snake women are also believed to be the most beautiful and alluring of all.

entrance everyone around them with their hypnotic gaze and sensual conversation. Once committed, Snakes are capable of deep and enduring love for their partners. Snakes are smart in the love arena, choosing partners according to perceived personal or social benefits. While they can often appear cold and aloof, this demonstration of emotional detachment is just part of their intricate plan of entrapment.

The Snake family member The stability and constancy of family and home provide Snakes with the structured and reliable environment they prefer. Snakes make good homemakers; they are gifted with money-management skills and will ensure that their families do not want for anything. Deeply attached to their partners and children, Snakes can be a little oversensitive and overprotective toward their loved ones. These traits are also evident in Snake children, who are very sensitive to family quarrels.

They are generally protective of their siblings, but don't like them gaining too much attention from their parents. This brings out their jealous streak.

The Snake friend Snakes are very sociable and are dedicated party-goers. They prefer controlled indoor activities and are fascinated by cultural pursuits. Hence they will spend much of their social time arranging and attending trips to theaters, galleries, and museums with their friends. Snakes appreciate the finer things in life and enjoy luxuriating in opulence. Fine dining and vintage wines are always popular with Snakes, who will hold many understated but exquisite dinner parties.

The Snake at work Snakes often find success later in life, as they spend their younger years cultivating their social and artistic interests. Once they become career oriented, Snakes demonstrate keen business acumen and political know-how. They won't necessarily seek obvious positions of power, preferring roles where they can quietly and privately influence and counsel those the public thinks of as powerful. Snakes are the best networkers of the zodiac. They have excellent organizational skills and are extremely efficient at everything they do. Snakes appear to achieve much with very little effort. Generally liked in the workplace, they can sometimes be accused of having a hidden agenda when dealing with others.

Ideal occupations for Snakes Scientist, academic, art or food critic, writer, poet, philosopher, human resource manager, interior designer

The five Snake types

WOOD SNAKES • 1965 • The presence of wood makes Snakes quite laid back and happy to indulge in their leisure and cultural pursuits, rather than focusing on their careers. Wood Snakes' occupations of choice will be ones that are sedate and independent—writing, for example. This will enable them to blend their work perfectly with their social and cultural activities.

FIRE SNAKES • 1917, 1977 • Fire Snakes are in their natural element, and this serves to accentuate their already impressive lists of traits. Fire Snakes will have far more energy and dynamic presence than other Snakes, and are likely to set many professional goals, which they will achieve with little effort.

EARTH SNAKES • 1929, 1989 • Earth balances the Snake's sometimes fragile inner peace, so Earth Snakes are more relaxed and openly communicative than other Snakes. They are calm and gentle people who are genuinely concerned about others. They are not as manipulative or secretive as other Snakes.

METAL SNAKES • 1941, 2001 • Metal brings unwavering strength and seriousness to Snakes' characters—Metal Snakes have a very healthy ego. Metal Snakes are confident in their own abilities and are perfectionists in everything they do. They are also ambitious and capable of working long and hard to achieve their goals.

WATER SNAKES • 1953, 2013 • Both water and Snakes are highly intuitive; the combination means that Water Snakes will be revered for their accurate perceptions and feelings. Some Water Snakes are naturally gifted with clairvoyance—they will at the least make highly valued counselors and advisors to business and political leaders.

Famous Snakes

MAHATMA GANDHI, POLITICAL/SOCIAL LEADER

Mahatma Gandhi displayed all the shrewdness, intuitiveness, and political savvy for which Snakes are famous. He was also a calm and caring person, which is a particular trait of Earth Snakes. Gandhi certainly used all the traits of his animal and element sign in his chosen profession.

RELATIONSHIP CHART FOR SNAKES

Snake +	Rating	Potential for harmony in love, friendship, and professional life
Ox	Best friend	Much happiness could come from this pairing. Oxen will provide Snakes with stability and with physical resources for meeting their common goals. Snakes will entice Oxen into lighter moods when necessary.
Rooster	Best friend	Each will complement and respect the other. Snake will admire Rooster's flamboyant social presence. Rooster will appreciate Snake's wise counsel and social refinement.
Rat	Positive	Each will challenge the other's mental abilities, ensuring that a satisfying relationship evolves where each can learn much from the other.
Tiger	Challenging	A one-sided attraction. Tiger won't be able to resist the aloof and enchanting Snake. However, the Snake will not be attracted to the tactless Tiger and will soon slither off to other, more elusive characters.
Rabbit	Good but needs work	Their common tact and political correctness will keep these two respecting each other. However, the secretive side to both these animals may lead to suspicion if open communication is not maintained.
Dragon	Positive	An extremely attractive match. Dragon will feel respected and socially elevated by Snake's beauty and social graces. Snake will be smart enough to appreciate Dragon's dynamic appeal.
Snake	Good but needs work	These two will have much hypnotic attraction to each other, but as Snakes can be secretive and jealous, it is best for their emotional well-being that two Snakes do not stay long together.
Horse	Challenging	A case of opposites attracting at first sight. Snake will be impressed with Horse's free spirit, and Horse will be attracted to Snake's charm. They will soon find little else to appreciate.
Sheep	Good but needs work	There will be enough mutual interest in art, music, and theater for these two to be friends. However, Sheep is quite sentimental and sensitive and will soon be put off by Snake's detachment.
Monkey	Positive	There is enough mental dexterity here to ensure success as business partners. Snake will provide the logic, and Monkey the willingness to take calculated risks.
Dog	Challenging	In the long run, this combination will work only with difficulty. Snake tends to be intense and secretive, and the honorable and up-front Dog is likely to see this as deceit.
Pig	Archenemy	Pigs are open and generous with their affection. Snakes are secretive and keep their feelings to themselves. Neither will be able to understand or respect the other.

SNAKE (NATIVE AMERICAN)

Snakes represent many things to Native Americans. First, they are seen as the ultimate transformative creatures, given their ability to shed their skins to suit their environments—this also demonstrates their superior survival skills. In addition, Snakes are prized for their sensual, hypnotic influence and are, therefore, often associated with physical desirability and procreation.

Snake people are said to have survived many trials in previous lives and, accordingly, to have earned the right to be linked to this auspicious animal totem. Surviving a snakebite is a sign of having passed a physical and/or spiritual test. Snake people are hardy, physically and mentally strong, and durable. They are life's real survivors and can return to strength and hope quickly after setbacks.

Their keen observation skills and sensory acuity give Snake people a degree of insight into other people and environments that few can match. Snakes are the most skilled catalysts of change—in people and in external events. However, Snake people are resistant to change themselves. They are determined and patient, and have intense self-control.

SEASON	The heart of fall—a time of early morning frosts and the coming of the cold
SEASON TOTEM	Grizzly Bear
SEASON ELEMENT	Earth
BIRTH TIME	October 23–November 21 Northern Hemisphere April 20–May 20 Southern Hemisphere
BIRTH TIME ELEMENT	Water
ELEMENTAL CLAN	Frog
ENERGY FLOW	Receptive
AFFINITIES	Color: orange Plant: thistle Mineral: copper
GIFTS	Patience, sensuality, ambition, charisma, wisdom, detachment, imagination, vitality
CHALLENGES	Jealousy, deceitfulness, stubbornness, critical nature
LIFE PATH	To take a dose of your own medicine regularly; to stop resisting changing yourself and to go within regularly to experience your own animal totem power of transformation.

Snake people do tend to have highly charged sex drives, often hinted at by their physical intensity, smoldering sensuality, and striking good looks. Meeting their sensual needs and fulfilling their desires takes a great deal of Snake people's physical and emotional energy. Snakes are ambitious, usually acquiring success and wealth easily. They are driven to accumulate things such as money and possessions, but they also like to accumulate new people and life experiences.

IDEAL PAIRINGS

Snake +	Relationship potential
Wolf	Wolf will be happy to let Snake take control in the relationship and will be thankful for Snake's wise counsel. Snake will be content with Wolf's selflessness.
Woodpecker	The relationship will be sensuous and mutually satisfying. Both Snake and Woodpecker have significant emotional needs that the other can meet.
Snow Goose	Sensuous Snake will ignite Snow Goose's primal energies. Snow Goose will keep all Snake's wavering principles and values in check.
Brown Bear	Both are patient and wise individuals who will be able to see the numerous benefits in the relationship before physical attraction has even taken hold.
Beaver	**Complement.** A natural attraction and kinship exists between these two animal totems. Each will make the other a loyal and supportive companion.

CHALLENGING PAIRINGS

Snake +	Relationship potential
Otter	Snake will constantly be jealous of Otter's popularity and will soon seek the limelight with other, less attractive companions.
Hawk	Snake is patient, while Hawk is rash. Neither will be able to understand the other's behavior. They will soon depart to find more compatible companions.
Deer	Snake can take the hard knocks in life, while Deer has a tendency to falter. Snake will think Deer weak, and Deer will think Snake too rigid and critical.
Salmon	Both are quite sensual, but Salmon is openly affectionate, while Snake will only demonstrate feelings in private. Over time, they will feel uncomfortable with each other.
Raven	Raven will be open to manipulation and deception when Snake turns on the charisma. Snake will soon tire of the game, and Raven will feel lucky to be out of the union.
Owl	Owl and Snake are rivals in any context, and a relationship will bring out the worst in both of them—jealousy and deceitfulness in Snake, pride and intolerance in Owl.
Snake	Snake pairing with another will bring about a mirroring effect, whereby the best and the worst in each other will be magnified.

SNOW GOOSE

The snow goose, a beautiful white bird with black-tipped wings, is quite gregarious, living and traveling in large flocks. Its migration pattern includes flying off to northern nesting grounds just as spring begins and returning with the first snows of late fall/early winter. Their return is a sign to Native Americans to prepare for the coming winter, an intense season requiring rest, cleansing, and renewal of the spirit. Snow geese are referred to as the "birds beyond the north winds."

Snow Goose people are referred to as the "keepers of old wisdoms." They are traditional, ritualistic, and serious, sometimes

appearing proper, stately, even reserved. However, they do like to be around others, provided social gatherings are for constructive purposes, as well as being opportunities to exercise their intelligence.

They have a strong code of conduct and keen vision, which ensures that they are meticulous and thorough in everything they do. They set high standards of performance for both themselves and others, which means that they sometimes come across as

SEASON	Early winter—a time when nature comes to rest and to renew itself
SEASON TOTEM	White Buffalo
SEASON ELEMENT	Air
BIRTH TIME	December 22–January 19 Northern Hemisphere June 21–July 22 Southern Hemisphere
BIRTH TIME ELEMENT	Water
ELEMENTAL CLAN	Frog
ENERGY FLOW	Receptive
AFFINITIES	Color: white Plant: birch tree Mineral: quartz
GIFTS	Gregariousness, enthusiasm, idealism, determination, perseverance, respect, thoroughness, seriousness, realism
CHALLENGES	Skepticism, arrogance, stubbornness, authoritativeness
LIFE PATH	To let go and be open to the new and unknown; to spend some time outside the usual routine, with no structure or expectation.

nit-picking and manipulative. Snow Geese are loyal and respect their family members, friends, and coworkers. They can truly keep confidences and will stand by and support family, friends, and coworkers through the roughest and darkest of times.

Some Snow Geese have a talent for storytelling—they have a vivid imagination and an ability to communicate clearly and concisely, and so can communicate in story form the ideals and customs that are important to them.

IDEAL PAIRINGS

Snow Goose +	Relationship potential
Beaver	Both are hardworking and practical-minded; hence, each will respect the other's loyalty and dedication throughout life.
Brown Bear	Both are dedicated and methodical individuals who will provide each other with the support and encouragement they desire for their endeavors.
Wolf	Snow Goose will be encouraged to develop spirituality through this association, and Wolf will be provided with direction and determination.
Snake	Sensuous Snake will ignite Snow Goose's primal energies. Snow Goose will keep all Snake's wavering principles and values in check.
Woodpecker	**Complement.** A natural attraction and kinship exists between these two animal totems. Each will make the other a loyal and supportive companion.

CHALLENGING PAIRINGS

Snow Goose +	Relationship potential
Otter	Both have air as their season element, which means they have similar lessons to learn in life. They can help each other—provided both are mature enough to respect their differences.
Hawk	Snow Goose will grow increasingly frustrated with Hawk's impatience. Hawk will find Snow Goose too stubborn and unwilling to change.
Deer	Snow Goose will find Deer superficial, and Deer will soon be dismissed. Deer will be too easily hurt by Snow Goose's arrogance.
Salmon	Both have extremely healthy egos, making it difficult for either to compromise.
Raven	Serious and authoritative Snow Goose will not be able to lift Raven's occasional depression. Snow Goose will see no value in the union.
Owl	Both will want to dominate the relationship and antagonism will build over time.
Snow Goose	Snow Goose pairing with another will bring about a mirroring effect, whereby the best and the worst in each other will be magnified.

T

TAURUS

APRIL 21 TO MAY 21
SYMBOL: THE BULL
RULING PLANET: VENUS
GROUPS: NEGATIVE, EARTH, FIXED

Yours is the most stable sign of the zodiac—you will stick to jobs and relationships as long as humanly possible. Being reliable, patient, tenacious, and conscientious, you are valued as a worker and you excel in any field in which you can use your hands and your creative talents.

Your career choices tend toward secure positions; you find satisfaction in working within large corporations. You can also cope well with routine. You are particularly good at running your own business, especially if you are partnered by a person who is content to take care of publicity and the day-to-day dealings with clients. Accounting, engineering, and agriculture are career choices that can appeal to you.

A major Taurean challenge is their famous obstinacy. Once they have decided on a particular career path or way of thinking, there is no convincing them of an alternative course of action. Some Taureans who have become well known in history for their obstinacy include Karl Marx and Vladimir Lenin. Taureans should be encouraged to learn flexibility and to be a bit more open-minded.

ASTROLOGICAL COMPATIBILITY

WHAT SUN SIGN ARE YOU? Taurus

WHO ARE YOUR FRIENDS? Cancer, Pisces

WHO ARE YOUR LOVERS? Virgo, Capricorn

You value a happy partnership more than anything, thriving on a sense of emotional security. Sometimes, by wanting this stability so much, you can be rather possessive about the time your partner spends away from you. You like closeness in your relationships and will usually be a very faithful companion.

Your home is important to you, so you do all you can to make it attractive and comfortable. Good-quality furnishings and fine art on the walls satisfies your love of beauty and gives you a sense of permanence and stability.

Beauty, grace, and elegance have been catchwords for some famous Taureans, such as Audrey Hepburn and Margot Fonteyn. Taureans are often considered the most attractive of the star signs in the zodiac. Some Taureans are attracted to working in areas that are luxurious or glamorous, such as beauty parlors and the film industry.

Many Taureans also show interest in using their voice and will join a choir or band. Some Taureans have achieved fame as musicians and singers—Ella Fitzgerald, Barbra Streisand, Bing Crosby, and Duke Ellington, for example.

You are surprisingly sociable and make friends easily, but friends are not as important to you as your family. You generally keep your friends for a long time and are considered a most sympathetic listener. Your children will always be well provided for, but you may need to make sure that you allow them some freedom, as your instincts may otherwise lead you to be rather a strict disciplinarian.

You like saving for a rainy day. A challenge for materialistic Taureans is to feel that they have enough money.

Taureans enjoy all the good things in life, including good food and wine. However, with their notoriously slow metabolisms, they need to implement lifelong strategies to manage potential weight problems. A balanced diet between dining extravaganzas, plus regular exercise, will help Taureans keep their figure.

TIGER

THE COURAGEOUS, DOMINANT TIGER
1914, 1926, 1938, 1950, 1962, 1974, 1986, 1998, 2010
ENERGY: YANG
ELEMENT: WOOD
TIME: 3:00 A.M.–5:00 A.M.
MONTH: FEBRUARY
DIRECTION: EAST/NORTHEAST
SEASON: EARLY SPRING

In China, the tiger is the king of the beasts. Those born under this sign have a magnetic, uplifting, motivating presence, and many of the qualities of a good leader.

Tiger people are born adventurers—they are optimistic daredevils. Full of excited expectation, they know only two speeds: full speed or stopped. They live for the moment, engaging in life passionately and with childlike excitement.

Generally lucky, most Tigers are able to triumph over all types of misadventure—which is important, as they tend to lead volatile lives. Tigers are freedom lovers and rule breakers. They demand plenty of space in their relationships and as few rules as possible in their daily lives.

The Tiger ascendant for those born between 3:00 A.M. **and 5:00** A.M.

Having the Tiger as the ascendant sign brings passion, courage, and conviction. These people will also find hidden strengths within themselves when they need to cope with loss or poor health.

Tigers at their best Brave, giving, charming, idealistic, bold, optimistic, passionate, independent

Tigers at their worst Reckless, impatient, disobedient, hotheaded, predatory, rebellious, aggressive, overly emotional

Character traits of Tigers Charismatic, bold, protective, generous, curious, lucky, courageous, optimistic, idealistic, determined, intelligent, sensitive, benevolent, ambitious, loyal, honorable, reckless

Life challenge for Tigers To learn to appreciate the benefits of patience and the wise counsel of others.

The Tiger lover Tigers are passionate in the extreme, with unquenchable sexual thirsts. They are born flirts who win their beloved's heart by performing heroic deeds and by arranging exciting and fun dates. Tigers' attraction to change and adventure leaves them with little time to settle down and marry. They like to experiment with short bursts of monogamy, but the monotony and routine soon stifle them, ensuring rather a promiscuous lifestyle in the long run.

The Tiger family member Adorable, energetic, and engaging as children, Tigers grow up to be the family's champion. Generous with their time, money, and possessions, they will not hesitate to give everything up to ensure the safety of even the most distant relative—and they never ask for anything back. Children are attracted to Tigers because they are fun loving. They are naturally good parents: quite protective, but also encouraging. Provided they are given their freedom and space to roam, most Tigers are capable of successfully establishing a family in middle or later life.

The Tiger friend Full of personality, humor, and unmatched optimism, Tigers make entertaining and uplifting friends. They love having a busy social life and can't resist the allure of parties. Gifted storytellers, they are a must at any social gathering and love to dress up. Tigers also make loyal and dependable friends who will stand by their mates during their ups and downs. As they can't stand lingering in misery themselves, they won't tolerate dark moods in others and will go to any lengths to brighten up everyone's day.

The Tiger at work Tigers make motivating managers and formidable leaders, and they quickly rise to positions of power. Their supremacy will be unmatched if they learn early to heed the counsel of those wiser and more reflective than themselves. Tigers are loyal to their employers and supportive of their colleagues. They are likely to take up many causes; they deplore workplace injustice. Ambitious and talented, Tigers are attracted to the recognition and rewards a job can give them.

Tiger's position as the third animal at Buddha's side denotes nobility and honor. In China, the tiger, not the lion, is believed to be king of all beasts. Those born under this sign display many leadership qualities and have a dynamic presence.

Ideal occupations for Tigers Entrepreneur, actor, writer, union leader, explorer, teacher, military leader

The five Tiger types

WOOD TIGERS • 1914, 1974 • The influence of double wood creates a very charming and socially oriented Tiger. Wood Tigers love to entertain and be entertained. They are the life of the party, preferring to keep to a carefree existence, free of any commitments.

FIRE TIGERS • 1926, 1986 • Fire adds even more passion and energy to Tigers' personalities. Fire Tigers are constantly chasing new opportunities and frequently changing careers. Their hectic and stressful lifestyles can cause early burnout.

EARTH TIGERS • 1938, 1998 • The influence of the earth element provides the daring Tiger with much-needed stability and practicality. Earth Tigers are the most patient of all Tigers and the most likely to succeed in balancing their lives and achieving their long-range goals. Earth Tigers have a strong nurturing side to their characters, making them indulgent parents and partners.

METAL TIGERS • 1950, 2010 • Loaded with added strength and vitality, Metal Tigers are the most ruthless and ambitious of all Tigers, rarely showing any sentimentality. They make commanding but inflexible figures in business and often have fierce tempers.

WATER TIGERS • 1962 • Water Tigers are the most intuitive and calm of all Tigers, which ensures them a less volatile life. They operate from highly tuned instincts, and their gut feelings about people and things are usually correct. They make fair and just leaders and are champions of life's underdogs.

Famous Tigers

HUGH HEFNER, PUBLISHER

Hugh Hefner is a Fire Tiger who displays this Tiger's double dose of passion and energy. Creating the Playboy empire from humble beginnings, Hefner has attracted much publicity and notoriety as a fast-living businessman, and has enjoyed many a love affair, a trait for which Tigers are famous.

JODIE FOSTER, ACTOR

Jodie Foster is a calmer Tiger. She has achieved the rare feat of successfully moving from child actor to a highly acclaimed adult actor. Water Tigers are intuitive and are gifted communicators. An acting career is an ideal choice of profession for these Tigers.

RELATIONSHIP CHART FOR TIGERS

Tiger +	Rating	Potential for harmony in love, friendship, and professional life
Horse	Best friend	A beneficial pairing, where each could provide the other with the freedom and fanfare they crave. Horses will encourage Tigers to pursue their dreams, and Tigers will reward Horses with lots of excitement.
Dog	Best friend	There will be much understanding and respect between these two. Practical Dogs will ease Tigers' impulsiveness, and energetic Tigers will chase away Dogs' anxieties and inner doubts.
Rat	Challenging	They have different perspectives on life, and their personal values and goals will clash. Any attraction will be only fleeting, with Rats more interested in material accumulation, and Tigers all for adventure.
Ox	Challenging	In the wild these two are natural enemies. Both are physically powerful and will want to dominate the relationship. This could lead to conflict and exhaustion on both parts.
Tiger	Good but needs work	A natural attraction, fueled by both being daring and both thirsting for adventure. With neither having much patience or practicality, though, a match of two Tigers would be reckless; in fact, it could be extremely dangerous.
Rabbit	Positive	Flexible Rabbits will be happy for Tigers to take the lead. Tigers will feel appreciated and supported, and Rabbits will feel encouraged to take bigger risks.
Dragon	Positive	These two have much in common and could live and work comfortably together. There will be opportunity for dynamic enterprise if both learn to respect each other's time in the limelight.
Snake	Challenging	A one-sided attraction. Tigers won't be able to resist the aloof and mesmerizing Snakes. However, Snakes won't be attracted to the tactless Tigers and will soon slither off.
Sheep	Good but needs work	Apart from their high sex drives, Sheep and Tigers will have little in common. Sheep will be hurt by Tigers' need for adventure and personal space. Tigers will soon feel smothered in this pairing.
Rooster	Good but needs work	Each will be attracted to the other's appearance, but they have very different communication styles. Rooster will henpeck Tiger on every detail, which will frustrate carefree Tiger to no end.
Pig	Positive	Home-loving Pigs will be happy and appreciative if Tigers act as providers and protectors. Tigers will bask in Pigs' admiration and indulgent nature.
Monkey	Archenemy	Both are competitive and impatient daredevils, ensuring many calamities if they pair up. Tiger will be supersensitive to Monkey's pranks, and Monkey will soon get bored with Tiger's lack of wisdom.

VIRGO

AUGUST 24 TO SEPTEMBER 22
SYMBOL: THE VIRGIN OR MAIDEN
RULING PLANET: MERCURY
GROUPS: NEGATIVE, EARTH, MUTABLE

Clever, conscientious, and thorough, you get the job done. You are usually a perfectionist, and you have the ability to focus on the details of a job. Virgoans have a strong sense of duty; their challenge is to not let duty destroy their joy of life. Nor should they limit their vision to merely the details—they need to look at the bigger picture.

Being attuned to mental rather than physical jobs, you love to work with ideas and with words. Famous Virgoan authors include Leo Tolstoy, D. H. Lawrence, and O. Henry. You often are attracted to a variety of interests and love learning about new concepts and theories. You are highly intelligent and need to be constantly active to ensure that you don't become bored.

You are more of a backroom person than a leader, but you need to be appreciated for the hard work you put in. One challenge faced by Virgoans is lack of confidence. This can lead them to be particularly critical—not only of themselves, but also of their loved ones. However, with some encouragement from family and friends, Virgoans can be coaxed to maintain their self-confidence; this will substantially reduce their need to criticize others.

ASTROLOGICAL COMPATIBILITY

♍

WHAT SUN SIGN ARE YOU? Virgo

WHO ARE YOUR FRIENDS? Cancer, Scorpio

WHO ARE YOUR LOVERS? Taurus, Capricorn

You have few important relationships, but you are intensely loyal to those who matter to you. You have a tendency to become withdrawn when disappointed by your loved ones and to become overly critical. As you are a perfectionist, your challenge is to accept that everyone, including yourself, can make mistakes, and that this is a valid way of learning how to live a full and rewarding life.

You prefer to show your love by doing things for your partner rather than by simply being affectionate. If you start to feel critical of your partner, try using your skills of perception on yourself—perhaps your response is coming from your own feelings of insecurity and weaknesses.

Your worst problems are fussiness and a tendency to worry unnecessarily about your health. However, your interest in health issues may lead you to adopt a career in the alternative health and healing industries. Generally your health will suffer if you do not have enough to do or to think about. You may suffer from depression and poor digestion if you are not happy with your life.

You are usually careful with money, apart from occasional binge spending on books and music, as financial security is very important to you. You dress carefully and with great neatness. You love clothes and accessories of good quality. Your home is often very ordered and clean, and the interior often reflects your many interests, as you tend to decorate your home with items that have caught your eye because of their beauty or uniqueness.

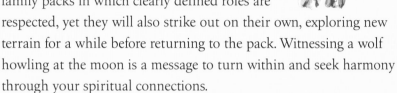

WOLF

Native Americans admire the wolf, seeing it as a fine example of the successful integration of individualism and family unity. Wolves live in family packs in which clearly defined roles are respected, yet they will also strike out on their own, exploring new terrain for a while before returning to the pack. Witnessing a wolf howling at the moon is a message to turn within and seek harmony through your spiritual connections.

Wolf people are prone to contradictions. For instance, they may become restless if little or no individual space and freedom are provided. They may also become stressed and worried if left on their own for too long. It's a constant tug-of-war that Wolves impose on themselves—a struggle between home and security, freedom and independence. This struggle is characterized by the season of their birth—late winter is a time of big, blustery winds.

Among some of the gifts Wolves possess are incredibly keen

SEASON	Late winter—a time of big, strong, blustery winds
SEASON TOTEM	White Buffalo
SEASON ELEMENT	Air
BIRTH TIME	February 19–March 20 Northern Hemisphere August 23–September 22 Southern Hemisphere
BIRTH TIME ELEMENT	Water
ELEMENTAL CLAN	Frog
ENERGY FLOW	Receptive
AFFINITIES	Color: blue–green Plant: plantain Mineral: turquoise
GIFTS	Creativity, intuitiveness, trustworthiness, loyalty, philosophical nature, spirituality, genuineness, selflessness
CHALLENGES	Restlessness, depression, nervousness, indecisiveness
LIFE PATH	To harness the emotional winds that can buffet you in many different physical directions and make you subject to many different moods.

senses. Their finely tuned instincts and sense of their environment and the people around them enable them to pick up messages very swiftly. If something or someone doesn't feel right, Wolves will quickly back away, often without being able to express exactly what it is that is making them feel uneasy.

Wolves are sensitive and can easily take offense and be hurt by the actions and words of others. This is particularly evident in their love life, which can be rocky at times. They need to temper this by seeking clarification and confirmation of others' intentions and by trying to control their reactions carefully.

IDEAL PAIRINGS

Wolf +	Relationship potential
Woodpecker	Given their emotion-centered approach to life, each will be sensitive and loyal to the other.
Snake	Wolf will be happy to let Snake take control in the relationship and will be thankful for Snake's wise counsel. Snake will be content with Wolf's selflessness.
Snow Goose	Snow Goose will be encouraged to develop spirituality through this association, and Wolf will be provided with direction and determination.
Beaver	Wolf will gain materialistically from a union with the industrious Beaver. Beaver will admire Wolf's philosophical and spiritual approach to life.
Brown Bear	**Complement.** A natural attraction and kinship exists between these two animal totems. Each will make the other a loyal and supportive companion.

CHALLENGING PAIRINGS

Wolf +	Relationship potential
Otter	Otter will fruitlessly endeavor to raise Wolf from melancholy states, while Wolf will fail to provide the support Otter requires for achieving goals.
Hawk	Hawk is impatient and impulsive, while Wolf is restless and indecisive. Neither will be able to make a decision that will make both happy.
Deer	Both can be extremely nervous types. They may experience high anxiety while in a relationship together.
Salmon	Salmon is likely to take advantage of Wolf's trusting heart. Wolf will soon leave the relationship wounded and depressed.
Raven	As neither are capable of making decisions in a relationship, nothing will be achieved. This could open the door to depression for both.
Owl	Owl will be frustrated and intolerant of Wolf's indecisiveness and sensitivity. Wolf will soon feel it better to go it alone.
Wolf	Wolf pairing with another will bring about a mirroring effect, whereby the best and the worst in each other will be magnified.

WOODPECKER

Woodpeckers are respected by Native Americans for their unique drumming behavior, which is believed to represent the beating of the heart. Hearing a woodpecker play its song out loud to the world is a sign to Native Americans to tune in to their own heart song and courageously follow its message.

Woodpecker people live their lives according to what they feel is right. They listen to their hearts rather than their minds, thus avoiding an overly logical approach to decision-making.

Woodpeckers are considered the most nurturing, charitable, and generous of all people. They are blessed with naturally strong principles and values, and they adhere to these in their everyday lives. They have an open mind about everyone they meet and an open heart for all. They are neither discriminatory nor distrusting.

To Woodpeckers, the whole world is just one large, extended family. They are particularly home-oriented. They value their relationships with others highly. As family and friends mean a lot to

SEASON	Early summer—a time of long, hot days
SEASON TOTEM	Coyote
SEASON ELEMENT	Water
BIRTH TIME	June 21–July 22 Northern Hemisphere December 22–January 19 Southern Hemisphere
BIRTH TIME ELEMENT	Water
ELEMENTAL CLAN	Frog
ENERGY FLOW	Receptive
AFFINITIES	Color: pink Plant: wild rose Mineral: carnelian
GIFTS	Intuition, loving nature, generosity, sensitivity, trust, devotion, loyalty, calmness
CHALLENGES	Vulnerability, insecurity, gullibility, anxiety
LIFE PATH	To take time each day to love and nurture yourself as much as you do others, and to stay true to yourself and what you feel is right.

Woodpeckers, they take their commitments seriously, generously opening their homes and giving of themselves and what they possess to ease the hardships of others. Woodpeckers thrive when in the company of others.

Woodpeckers are also quite naturally intuitive and sensitive to their environment and those around them. They are particularly good in a crisis, when their calm and caring approach is much appreciated.

IDEAL PAIRINGS

Woodpecker +	Relationship potential
Snake	The relationship will be sensuous and mutually satisfying. Both Snake and Woodpecker have significant emotional needs that the other can meet.
Wolf	Given their emotion-centered approach to life, each will be sensitive and loyal to the other.
Beaver	Woodpecker's loving nature and devotion will be enough to soften the usually inflexible nature of Beaver, who will reward Woodpecker with material security.
Brown Bear	There will be an immediate attraction—Brown Bear will be unable to resist Woodpecker's generous and loyal nature, and Woodpecker will enjoy Brown Bear's courage and perseverance.
Snow Goose	**Complement.** A natural attraction and kinship exists between these two animal totems. Each will make the other a loyal and supportive companion.

CHALLENGING PAIRINGS

Woodpecker +	Relationship potential
Otter	Both lack drive and ambition; hence, neither will be able to help the other in productive endeavors.
Hawk	These two operate at different levels. Hawks are bold and independent, while Woodpeckers are introverted and dependent. Neither will have their needs met in this relationship.
Deer	Both are prone to nervousness and insecurity. Theirs would be a vulnerable relationship, lacking in any real support and practicality.
Salmon	Woodpeckers like to stay at home and cuddle, while Salmon would rather go out and party. Each will go their own way in time.
Raven	Woodpecker will be too sensitive and vulnerable to Raven's confusion and indecision. Raven will find Woodpecker lacking in energy and inspiration.
Owl	Owl is too self-reliant for Woodpecker to feel any true union between them. Owl will not find Woodpecker stimulating company.
Woodpecker	Woodpecker pairing with another will bring about a mirroring effect, whereby the best and the worst in each other will be magnified.

GLOSSARY AND SUGGESTED READING

ACTIVE In Chinese astrology, like yang. In animal totem astrology, this energy is associated with the Sun and conscious activity, linked to the elements of fire and air; the animal totems with either fire or air as their birth time element demonstrate active energy in their general behavior.

AFFINITIES In animal totem astrology, these are the specific minerals and plants associated with each birth time; acquiring and using them can add further strength to an animal totem's specific power and medicine.

ANIMAL TOTEM An animal symbol representing a birth time, season, or element of nature.

ASCENDANT The exact degree of the rising sign. In Chinese astrology, this is the animal sign ruling the time of birth.

ASPECT The angles at which planets are placed relative to one another.

ASTROLOGY The study of the stars.

ASTRONOMY The science of the celestial bodies, their motions, positions, distances, magnitudes, etc.

BIRTH TIME ELEMENT The element of nature ruling a birth time.

BIRTH TOTEM The animal representing a birth time.

DESCENDANT The sign opposite your rising sign.

DESTINY CALENDAR The Aztec religious and predictive calendar, which is based on the movement of the stars and planets.

DOMINANT ANIMAL In Chinese astrology, this is the animal sign ruling the year of your birth.

DOMINANT ELEMENT In Chinese astrology, this is the element ruling the year of your birth.

ECLIPTIC The apparent path of the Sun.

ELEMENT Energies that indicate nature's influence on the astrological signs of various systems. In the West, these elements are fire, earth, air, and water. The Chinese elements are wood, fire, earth, metal, and water.

ELEMENTAL CLAN The animal group you belong to, given your birth time element.

ENERGY FLOW Energy flows through life in two complementary ways: actively and receptively. It is the flow of energy that gives force to the elements of earth, fire, air, and water. Each of the birth totems has either an active or a receptive energy flow; knowing the type will help you understand how each totem behaves.

FORTUNES In Arabic astrology, these are sensitive spots on a natal chart, each of which is associated with a specific area of one's life.

GEOMANCY The study of the geography of a region or marks in sand or earth for purposes of divination.

HOROSCOPE A forecast of a person's future derived from a study of the relative positions of the Sun, Moon, planets, and zodiacal constellations at the time of the person's birth.

LOVE SIGN In Chinese astrology, this is the animal sign ruling the month of your birth.

MANSIONS OF THE MOON *see* Nakshastras.

MEDICINE WHEEL A diagram illustrating the circular motion of life: the seasons, the forces of nature, and the powerful totems and affinities associated with each season.

MIDHEAVEN In Western, Arabic, and Vedic astrology, this is the part of a chart that points toward the place where the Sun is at its highest, i.e., toward the equator. It refers to a person's aims, ambitions, and worldly aspirations.

MIDPOINTS A midpoint is exactly halfway between two planets or other features on a horoscope. This may be the halfway mark between the ascendant and Venus, or Pluto and Mars, or the midheaven and Jupiter, and so forth.

NADIR This is exactly opposite the midheaven, around the back of the Earth, and furthest from where the Sun was at its highest when a person was born. It refers to a person's private life, home, family, and background.

NAKSHASTRAS The Mansions of the Moon, twenty-seven divisions of the zodiac that are similar to signs of the zodiac. These are used in Vedic astrology, but they also exist in Arabic, Chinese, and Roman astrology.

NATIVE AMERICANS The earliest human inhabitants of North America.

NATURAL ELEMENT In Chinese astrology, this is the element normally associated with each animal sign.

PURE SIGN In Chinese astrology, this occurs when the same animal sign rules both the year and the time of birth. In animal totem astrology, pure signs are animal totems for which the same element—air, earth, fire, or water—governs both the season and the birth time. Otter is pure air, Hawk is pure fire, and Woodpecker is pure water; no animal totem is pure earth.

QUALITY The groups of signs in Western astrology that are cardinal, fixed, or mutable. Cardinal signs are go-getters, fixed signs uphold the status quo, and mutable signs bring change and closure.

RECEPTIVE In Chinese astrology, like yin. In animal totem astrology, this energy is associated with the Moon and unconscious activity; linked to the elements of earth and water. The animal totems with either earth or water as their birth time element demonstrate receptive energy in their general behavior.

RISING SIGN The sign of the zodiac that is rising where day is breaking.

RUNES Letters of the Saxon, Teutonic, Viking, and Norse alphabets. The names of these vary according to which tradition is followed.

SEASON ELEMENT In animal totem astrology, the element ruling the season in which a person is born; sometimes referred to as the "principal element."

SEASON TOTEM In animal totem astrology, the animal totem representing the season in which a person is born; sometimes referred to as the "directional totem."

SHAMAN A tribal wise man or holy man with the power and skills to interpret the messages between the spirit and natural worlds and among the animal, mineral, and plant kingdoms.

SOLAR CALENDAR The Toltec, Mayan, and Aztec agricultural calendar.

THEBAIC CALENDAR Ancient Egyptian astrology.

VEDIC ASTROLOGY The astrology of the Indian subcontinent, including Sri Lanka, Pakistan, and related countries.

VERTEX A point on a chart that specifically refers to relationships with others. These would be the kind of relationships that are important and that a person is unlikely ever to forget.

YANG AND YIN The forceful, masculine (yang) or enduring, feminine (yin) energies of Chinese systems.

ZODIAC The constellations of stars along the ecliptic that we know by the names Aries, Taurus, etc.

SUGGESTED READING

Bryant, P., *The Aquarian Guide to Native American Mythology*, The Aquarian Press/HarperCollins, London, 1991.

Choy, H. & Henwood, B., *Feng Shui*, Lansdowne Publishing, Sydney, 1997.

Craze, R., *The Chinese Astrology Handbook*, Lorenz Books, London, 1998.

Fenton, S., *How to Read Your Star Signs*, HarperCollins, Sydney, 1998.

Fenton, S., *The Hidden Zodiac*, Stirling/Zambezi Publishing, UK, 2002.

Fenton, S., *Secrets of Chinese Divination*, Stirling/Zambezi Publishing, UK, 2003 (or via sasha@zampub.com).

Giles, B. & The Diagram Group, *Collins Gem Chinese Astrology*, HarperCollins, Glasgow, 1996.

Kennedy, M., *Native American Myth & Legend*, Blandford/Cassell, London, 1996.

Kwok, Man-Ho, *Authentic Chinese Horoscopes*, Arrow Books, London, 1987.

Lau, K., *Secrets of Chinese Astrology*, Tenyu Books, New York, 1994.

Lau, T., *The Chinese Horoscopes Guide to Relationships*, Souvenir Press, London, 1995.

Lau, T., *The Handbook of Chinese Horoscopes*, 3rd ed., Souvenir Press, London, 1995.

Lawson, D., *So You Want to Be a Shaman*, Conari Press & Publishers Group West, California, 1996.

Luxon, B., *Chinese Astrology*, Greenwich Editions, London, 1998.

McNeese, T., *Illustrated Myths of Native America*, Blandford/Cassell, London, 1998.

Meadows, K., *The Little Library of Earth Medicine*, Dorling Kindersley, London, 1998.

Mengelkoch, L. & Nerburn, K., *Native American Wisdom*, New World Library, San Rafael, California, 1991.

Moondance, W., *Spirit Medicine*, Sterling Publishing Company, New York, 1995.

Sams, J. & Carson, D., *Medicine Cards*, Bear & Company, Santa Fe, New Mexico, 1988.

Somerville, N., *Your Chinese Horoscope 1998*, Thorsons, London, 1997.

Summer Rain, M., *Earthway*, Pocket Books, New York, 1990.

Sun Bear and Wabun, *The Sun Bear Book of the Medicine Wheel*, Simon & Schuster, Sydney, 1980.

Sun Bear and Wabun, *The Medicine Wheel: Earth Astrology*, Fireside/Simon & Schuster, New York, 1982.

Sun Bear, Wabun, Wind & Mulligan, *Crysalis, Dancing with the Wheel*, The Medicine Wheel Workbook, Fireside/Simon & Schuster, New York, 1992.

Too, L., *Chinese Astrology for Romance & Relationships*, Konsep Books, Malaysia, 1996.

Walters, D., *Chinese Love Signs*, S. Abdul Majeed & Co., Malaysia, 1994.

Wherry, J. H., *The Totem Pole Indians*, Wilfred Funk, Inc., New York, 1964.

White S., *The New Astrology*, Pan Books, London, 1987.

White, S., *The New Chinese Astrology*, Pan Books, London, 1994.

INDEX